D0128372

# The
# HAM BOOK

## A Comprehensive Guide to Ham Cookery
### By Monette R. Harrell and Robert W. Harrell, Jr.

 Donning Company/Publishers
Norfolk

*To Our Parents*
*Mr. and Mrs. James Monroe Roberson, Sr.*
*Mr. and Mrs. Robert Wesley Harrell, Sr.*
*and*
*To Our Daughters*
*Robyn Monet and Cheri Renee*

THE COVER WAS PHOTOGRAPHED one lovely spring day on the grounds of St. John's Church, an Episcopal Church built in 1755 near Chuckatuck Village in Suffolk, Virginia. It overlooks Meadowbrook farm, the home of Mrs. W. G. Saunders, Jr. The formal buffet features Virginia Ham and delicious accompaniments: *Watermelon Pickle, Pickled Peaches, Homemade Cucumber Pickle, Tomato Aspic Loaf, Sherried Jelly with Pecan Balls, Sweet Potato Fluff, Peanut Pie,* and Burgundy.

Copyright©1977 by Monette R. Harrell and Robert W. Harrell, Jr.

All rights reserved, including the right to reproduce this book in any form whatsoever without permission in writing from the publisher, except for brief passages in connection with a review. For information write, The Donning Company/Publishers, Inc., 253 West Bute Street, Norfolk, Virginia 23510.

Library of Congress Cataloging in Publication Data:

Harrell, Monette R     1942-
The ham book.

Includes index.
1. Cookery (Ham)   2. Ham.   I. Harrell,
Robert W. Jr., 1939-      joint author.   II. Title.
TX749.H23        641.6'6'4        77-1233
ISBN 0-915442-14-0

Printed in the United States of America

Illustrations by Nancy Simpson Hoke
Cover design by Edward A. Conner

First Printing October 1977
Second Printing November 1977
Third Printing April 1978

# Contents

This smokehouse, probably built in the late 1700s, is on the Berry Hill Farm near Smithfield, Virginia, which has been in the Thomas L. Dashiell family for three generations.

# INTRODUCTION

*The Ham Book* is quite a unique cookbook. It contains only recipes that use ham as one of the ingredients or recipes that complement ham.

The diversity of ways that ham can be used extends beyond any one person's imagination. However, traditionally, ham sandwiches and sliced ham have been the major extent of its use by most homemakers for whom the concerned plea is, "What do I do with all my leftover ham?" This book is the answer to getting the most out of your ham and making your ham dollar count; for today, buying a ham is a real investment. *The Ham Book* is a collection of recipes that reflects the vivid imagination and creativity which many people have had in using ham.

My interest in collecting ham recipes first began when I married Robert Harrell, whose family has been in the Virginia ham business since 1898. This interest was further developed when Robert and I made several guest appearances on local television talk shows. As a result of these appearances, we received numerous letters requesting the televised ham recipes. Further demonstrating a genuine interest, many people sent in their own ideas and thus continued an exciting, growing collection, of which this book is the result.

Most of these recipes have been tested with Smithfield or Virginia ham, but unless a specific type of ham is indicated, any ham will make a delicious substitute. Always taste before adding salt since saltiness is one of the most important distinctions among types of ham.

Monette R. Harrell

# PART I
# HAM'S HERITAGE

# HISTORY OF HAM

The history of ham is filled with stories and folklore that add color to the legacy of what the dictionary defines as the hinder part of a pig's thigh that has been salted and smoked. Though it has proved impossible to document, the origin of the word could possibly have come from biblical times.

According to one version Ham, son of Noah, was the father of Canaan. The boy Canaan was extremely fond of his father, and in his ecstasy over an experiment in curing the thigh of a hog he christened the achievement in a spirit of affectionate regard for his father, by the name of ham. Thus the choicest food from hogs got an early introduction into the world. Since this early naming of that part of the pork carcass, ham has been synonymous with good eating.

In his early nineteenth century essay "A Dissertation of a Roast Pig" Charles Lamb describes Bobo, son of Ha-ti, who tasted the first roasted pig in Ancient China. Bobo's discovery of a burnt pig was quite by accident. He had been left in the care of his father's cottage while the father was away one morning. Being fond of playing with fire, Bobo let some sparks escape into a bundle of straw and burned down the house. While trying to pull a burnt pig from the rubble, he burned his fingers and quickly applied them to his mouth to cool them. The taste was so delicious that he tried again and again until his stomach was filled with this new found delicacy...roast pig. Thus began the cooking of pork.

Through the ages pork has been a favorite meat. Pigs have probably been domesticated for centuries (some estimates suggest since 7000 B.C.), and excavations in China show the breeding of pigs by about 1500 B.C. The Chinese considered pigs valuable assets and used them not only for their exceptional nutritional value, but also as sacrifices to the spirits on ceremonial occasions and as payment for the dowry of a young bride. The importance of the pig to Chinese culture is evident through their ideograph symbol for "home," which includes the signs for "pig" and for "roof."

The Greeks also considered pork to be a nutritious meat, and Hippocrates, circa 460 B.C., mentioned in his writing his belief that pork provided more strength than other types of meat. Roast pork was on the menu in the *Iliad*. The Romans considered wild boar a favorite delicacy, and many a victory was celebrated with a roasted pig as the focal point for the feast.

Controversy continues over the origin of the procedures for curing hams. Undoubtedly the intention was to preserve the meat, and the flavor now so highly regarded was a bonus. The ancient Gauls are purported to have salted, smoked and dried pork, and an annual ham fair was a pre-nineteenth century Paris tradition. Areas of Italy, France, Denmark, Poland, Britain, Germany, and the United States make proud claims about the quality and distinctiveness of their regional hams. The variety of types of ham and the diversity of their usefulness is evident not only in the *International Cookery* section of this book, but in the adaptability of the different hams to the recipes throughout *The Ham Book*.

Ham has become an American tradition and a part of the folklore of our times. Besides being served at special commemorative occasions, a ham has also become one man's pet. P. D. Gwaltney, Jr., cured a large Smithfield Ham in 1902, and since that time it has never been under refrigeration. It is today probably the oldest piece of edible cured meat in existence. On April 8, 1929, Ripley's "Believe It Or Not" reported that the ham was insured for a thousand dollars.

Mr. Gwaltney had a brass collar placed around the hock that read, "Mr. Gwaltney's Pet Ham," and in 1934 he took the "Pet Ham" to Washington with him to the American Bankers Association Convention. Quite a stir was created when he asked the desk clerk at the hotel to put his suitcase in the hotel vault. The desk clerk inquired as to what was in the suitcase, and Mr. Gwaltney explained that it was his "Pet Ham" which was insured for five thousand dollars. The next day a Washington paper carried the story about Mr. Gwaltney and his "Pet Ham." Today it is still insured for the same value and continues to sport the brass collar.

In colonial America, hams were part of the cuisine of Puritan New England and of the Virginia colonists. The brine-filled pork barrel was a staple of the New England cellar, and the smokehouse, either as part of the kitchen hearth or as a separate building, was a Southern specialty. It was believed that the type of wood used in the smoking process affected the flavor.

The two most important buildings on the early plantations were the smokehouse and the icehouse, for these were the buildings in which food was stored. Modern technology and the invention of the refrigerator replaced the icehouse, but in rural America you still find the family smokehouse, usually constructed of wood or brick, with an earthen floor and a cedar shake roof with ventilators in the eaves to let the smoke out. When one visits the early plantations of Jefferson and Washington at Monticello and Mount Vernon, the smokehouse is always pointed out with pride for it is definitely a part of the American architectural and gastronomic heritage.

Throughout recorded culinary history, cooks have been in constant research of better ways of preparing and preserving the succulent natural flavor that pork possesses. The English thought their York ham the *coup de grace* until the colonists at Jamestown began shipping Virginia hams to England in the 1600s.

Pigs were not native to the Jamestown area, but were brought to the colonies of Virginia from England and Bermuda and bred for food and the sport of wild boar hunting. The climate of Virginia and the abundant rich natural foods found there were perfect for the raising of swine, which multiplied and became very plentiful. So plentiful, in fact, that they became a nuisance to the settlers who rounded them up and placed them on an island in the James River halfway between Jamestown and what is now the town of Smithfield. This island became known as "Hog Island."

In 1608 Captain John Smith, who was commanding the James River settlement, sent a detachment across the river from the fort to search for food in the forest. As they foraged, the group came to a clearing in the woods, where they saw Indians smoking venison over a fire. Later they learned that smoking preserved the meat for winter use and protected it from foreign substances and insects. The settlers further learned that the Indians had rubbed the meat in what they termed "magic white sand" and left it for a while before smoking.

The "magic white sand" or "salt," as we know it, was obtained by boiling and evaporating the salt from sea water. The Indians also traded for salt with mountain tribes that dug it from the sides of hills, for it was extremely important to their existence. A number of the caves in the mountains of Virginia, Pennsylvania, and New York are believed to have been made by Indians searching for salt with which to preserve their food.

With its ability to preserve meats and other foods, salt has been the motivator of battles in the American Revolution and the Civil War, for it was essential to the preservation of food for troop movements. The battle of Fort Ticonderoga was fought over the control of salt mines in that area of New York, and in December 1864 Union forces made a forced march and staged a thirty-six hour battle to capture Saltville, Virginia, and thus cut off the South's salt supply.

A story circulating in Virginia's Roanoke Valley suggests that the salty hams of the rural South helped to ward off Yankee plundering of farms and villages during the Civil War. One Southern family hid their hams in their well, and blue-coated soldiers stopping for a drink found the water to have a strange odor and flavor. To the soldiers' questions about these peculiar qualities, the kitchen maid replied, "You shouldn't drink that water! We drop dead cats and every ol' thing down that well." The Northern soldiers made a speedy retreat, and the victorious Southern family brought up their hams to dry in the afternoon sun.

The curing of the Virginia ham is a meticulous process and the modern version is done under rigid control and timing with salt still the main ingredient. The ancient formula, adapted to the use of preserving the meat from wild boar and hogs, was passed from generation to generation. From the plantation days of old Virginia until the present, hickory-smoked Virginia country hams have been the hallmark of hospitality and delicious eating. Royal Governor William Bullock was praising the hams cured in Virginia as superior to those of his native England as early as 1649, and William Byrd included a recipe for Virginia ham among his other writings about his colonial home.

The Smithfield version of the legend of Pocahontas suggests that the Indian princess intervened to save Captain John Smith from the wrath of her father Powhatan because he was the only man who knew the correct way to cure a ham. Captain Smith was a relative of the founder of Smithfield, and, as with most legends, you can form your own opinion as to the validity of the Smithfield variation of this romantic tale.

Henry Howe, nineteenth century writer, says of Colonial Virginia, "Hogs swarming like vermin, ran at large in troops. It was the best poor man's country in the world. If a happy peace be settled in poor England, then they in Virginia shall be as happy a people as any under heaven." These wild hogs were the principal food of the new settlers, as well as of the Indians, because they were available all the year around and were more easily gotten than the water fowl that enlivened the morasses, the game in the forest or the covies of quail and wild turkeys which rustled in the woods. The early settlers preferred their Indian pork to any other and stuck to it. The razorback hogs to which Howe refers hung around until later years, developed into the aristocratic swine with the aristocratic taste of a gamey pork product.

In 1929 Will Rogers referred to Virginia as the producer of only three things—rattlesnakes, presidents, and razorbacks. In reply, the Virginia Chamber of Commerce shipped him a cooked Virginia ham to let him know the Commonwealth was also famous for its hams.

The major centers of curing hams are Suffolk, Smithfield, Richmond, and Southampton. All of these are within fifty miles of Jamestown, where it all originated. The international renown of the town of Smithfield has become synonymous with the dry salt smoked ham that is cured in Virginia.

Smithfield was named for Arthur Smith, upon whose land the town was first established, and by 1783 the exporting of hams from this port on the Pagan Creek was an important element in the economy of the area. Smithfield ham had become so famous in the early part of the twentieth century that in 1926 the Virginia General Assembly passed a law to protect it from imitation. The statute read: "Genuine Smithfield Hams are those cut from the carcasses of peanut-fed hogs, raised in the peanut belt of the State of Virginia or the State of North Carolina, and which are cured, treated, smoked and processed in the town of Smithfield, in the State of Virginia."

A company headed by Mallory Todd was one of the first companies to produce Virginia hams in quantity in Smithfield, beginning before 1779. Hams cured by the Todd family found their way to the royal dinner table at Windsor Castle during the reign of Queen Victoria, and Virginia ham still graces the table of Queen Elizabeth II, who was introduced to the product during her visit to the Jamestown Exposition in 1957.

Over the years it has been a tradition to exchange prize hams as barter for other items. Having a cured country ham in the smokehouse was

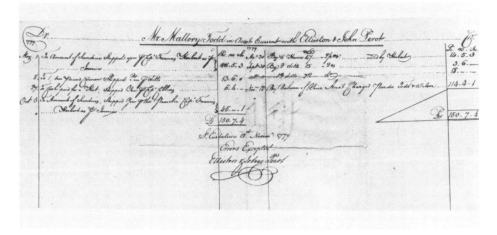

The above picture shows an invoice dated 1779, the first known commercial export sale of Virginia ham. It was sold to Elliston and John Perot on the Island of St. Eustatius. Among other items received in exchange for the ham were a two pound cannon and a hat.

like having money in the bank, and it could be traded for the necessities of life. In Grandfather Harrell's day farmers would bring their country hams to the General Merchandise Store in exchange for items ranging from dry goods to chocolate. The Barter Theatre in Abingdon, Virginia, still accepts a ham in exchange for admission to its plays. This tradition began during the 1930s when many people could afford to see plays only by exchanging ham and other foodstuffs for tickets. The late Bob Porterfield, founder of the theatre, created this concept in order to feed the actors and actresses and give them work during the depression years.

The heritage of centuries of curing and smoking hams in Virginia is focused on the distinctive savory taste, part of the inheritance left by the tiny band of settlers at Jamestown, that is still an important part of our American culinary tradition. The lavish entertainment of the colonial period featured this unique meat, whose flavor

still cannot be matched, and no Virginia hostess would consider her party a success without Virginia ham biscuits gracing her table.

Virginia ham has become a tradition not only of Virginia, but the United States. General Pershing served Virginia ham at an important banquet in Paris after World War I, and it was ordered by the United States government to be served in Berlin at the four power dinner celebrating the end of World War II. Today, over two million hams of all kinds are consumed each week in the United States.

Over the years, certain traditions connected with the curing of hams have become part of the folklore associated with the product.

As research and modern technologies have replaced family hand-me-down recipes, it has become apparent that many items and processes used to cure ham in earlier times have now become the traditions of a bygone era.

Advertising logos often claim that

the hams have the fragrance of the hickory logs or applewood over which they are smoked. The truth is that any type of hardwood serves the purpose; red oak is used in smoking the greatest proportion of hams cured in Virginia. The smoking process seals the exterior surface of a ham and offers a buffer and a preservative against foreign substances that might cause flavor deterioration. The smoke does leave a fragrance on the exterior surface, but it does not penetrate to the interior, for as the ham is heated and smoked, juices and moisture seep from the product. It is only the smoke on the exterior surface that gives the flavor of smoke to the meat. The heat is equally important as the smoke because it helps to dry the moisture from the exterior fat, thus reducing rancidity.

Black pepper was applied to the exterior surface of hams in earlier times in order to keep insects away. It is now expected on a Country-cured ham, even though the threat of insect infestation is absent from modern kitchens.

The old cloth bag which often enclosed hams in days gone by is another tradition; these wrappers found their way to old age as stuffed pillows, clothespin bags, and dish towels. The biggest complaint about the new plastic bags is that the juice and pulp cannot be strained through them when making grape jelly.

It is only the salt reacting with the natural flavor already in the ham, under proper conditions, that gives the distinct flavor that we have come to expect in a Virginia ham. While hickory smoke, pepper coating and cotton bags are part of the romance of this savory meat, they lend color of legend and memory rather than flavor to the ham.

## The Most Expensive Christmas Ham

The traditional Christmas ham is a delicious and economical way to impress special guests, but on occasion may be very costly. Rufus Walters, a friend and neighbor, purchased a large Smithfield ham for twenty dollars, and took it home for his wife to prepare for holiday guests. After cooking and preparing the ham in finest Virginia tradition, Mrs. Walters placed it on the back porch to cool before she would remove the skin and coat the ham with a brown sugar glaze.

The Walters owned a basset hound named Delilah, who was pregnant and very close to the time that she would have puppies. Delilah was let out on the back porch as usual. Alas! The aroma of a fine Virginia ham just removed from the oven was too great a temptation. Yes, it happened! Delilah nudged open the roaster and began to devour the ham.

Later that afternoon, groans were heard from the porch. The Walterses found Delilah lying on her side moaning, as any mammal would do after eating twelve pounds of meat. The cause of the moans was easily discovered, for nearby was an overturned roaster and a clean ham bone.

Fearing for Delilah's life and the welfare of her unborn puppies, Rufus quickly gathered up his overstuffed basset hound and proceeded to their friendly veterinarian, who informed them that a caesarean operation was necessary. It was accomplished at a cost of seventy-five dollars.

On the way home, Rufus realized there was no ham awaiting the guests and certainly not enough time to prepare another one. He circled by the ham plant and purchased a cooked ham costing twenty-five dollars. This, of course, brought the grand total of preparing the Christmas ham to one hundred and twenty dollars. However, all ended well on Christmas day except the bank account, for the guests were served a fine Virginia ham, and Delilah and puppies were doing fine in Dr. Kress's Animal Hospital.

# TYPES OF HAMS

Fresh ham is the uncured hind leg, cut from the hog at a temperature normally between 36° to 40° Fahrenheit, and is still in its natural fresh pork state.

**Dry-corned ham** is a fresh ham which has been rubbed externally with salt and allowed to remain in the salt for 7 to 10 days at 40° Fahrenheit.

**Wet-corned ham** is a fresh ham which has been artery pumped to 110 percent of the fresh ham's weight with a solution of salt and water by means of an instrument called a ham pump. The ham is then coated lightly with dry salt; it is cured in 24 hours.

**Tenderized, sugar-cured, packer's or smoked hams** have been artery pumped to 110 to 120 percent of the fresh ham's weight with a curing solution that generally contains salt, sodium nitrite, sodium nitrate, sodium ascorbate, sodium eryothobate, and sugar. The hams then hang at room temperature for four hours and are smoked until the internal temperature reaches 137° Fahrenheit and the exterior has reached the desired pinkish-red color. The hams return to their original weight during the smoking process. This ham can also be bought fully cooked, which means the ham's internal temperature has reached 155° Fahrenheit. This ham will be labeled fully cooked "Ready to Eat."

**Water-added smoked hams** are prepared by the same technique as tenderized sugar-cured hams but with a higher percentage of the solution. During the smoking process they do not return to their original weight. These hams are also available fully cooked and "Ready to Eat."

**Boned and rolled ham** is a smoked ham with the bones removed, pressed in a round synthetic casing to give it shape. It is fully cooked until the ham's internal temperature has reached 155° Fahrenheit. The slices can be broiled, baked, or fried.

**Boiled ham** is prepared like the water-added hams through the pumping stage; after the curing solution is injected, the bones are removed and the ham is placed in a stainless steel mold (usually 4 by 4 inches or 4 by 6 inches). The ham loaves are then fully cooked in a vat of water until an internal temperature of 160° is reached. They are not boiled, but simmered to enhance the ham flavor. Boiled ham can be purchased sliced by the pound or vacuum sealed in plastic packages.

**Westphalian ham** is not really a ham, but a 4 to 6 pound center muscle section of a shoulder butt, cured like smoked ham by an injection of brine solution and then smoked until an inside temperature of 137° Fahrenheit is reached.

**Prosciutto** is a highly seasoned

Italian style dry-cured pressed ham which is similar to Virginia, Country style, or Smithfield ham. Prosciutto is the Italian word for ham, and the famous uncooked version is actually from Parma. It has the aitch bone removed, salt and spices are applied to the exterior, and then it is placed under weights to press it flat. The length of the process and the amount of salt used make the ham safe to eat without cooking. The hams are sliced paper thin, either lengthwise or along the grain, and eaten uncooked. This type of ham is sold mostly in specialty food shops or in delicatessens.

**Smoked Country ham** is a dry salted aged ham that is cured mostly in the southern United States. The fresh hams are placed in salt for 28 to 35 days, the salt is removed from the hams by washing, and they are hung to dry for 14 days. The hams are then smoked with hardwood sawdust at 110° Fahrenheit and then hung to age in a 75° to 80° room until the burgundy red color and fragrant aroma are fully developed. The hams are then coated with pepper and are usually sold in cloth bags.

**Air-dried Country ham,** nonsmoked, is prepared by the same process as the smoked Country ham through the salty stage. After the salt is washed off, they are placed in an 80° room at 65 percent relative humidity and aged, generally for 40 days.

**Smithfield or Virginia ham** is a dry-salted, smoked ham that has a long shank, cut below the stifle joint on the hock end and on the butt end cut two and one half vertebrae up the spine. The skin is left on the entire back of the ham. The skin and fat protect the meat on the butt end from becoming excessively dry and hard. Cured by the same method as the Country ham, it is recognized by its distinct cut and age. During the curing and the six to twelve month aging process, the ham has a 25 to 30 percent moisture loss. This causes the percentage of salt to increase, giving the ham a saltier flavor and a deep rich burgundy color. This type of ham is also available fully cooked and ready to eat.

Virginia hams are cured in modern processing plants by the following method: Fresh hams are sprinkled with two ounces of sodium nitrate per 100 pounds of meat and coated with 20 pounds of salt per 100 pounds of meat and placed in bins that are stored in a 40° Fahrenheit room for 28 to 35 days depending on the weight range. Sodium nitrate is an essential ingredient to prevent botulism; it combines with the meat fibers to give the red interior color. They are overhauled (resalted) once after 5 days in the process. The salt is washed off the hams in 100° water and the hams are netted and hung in a 55° room for 14 days. The hams are then moved into a 110° smokehouse until they have developed a deep auburn color. From the smoking area, they are moved to an aging room where they age at 75° to 80° until they have developed that distinctive flavor and internal color that is synonymous with a quality Virginia ham.

During this curing process, the ham loses twenty percent of its moisture, twelve percent in the salting stage, two percent in the equalization stage and six percent in the smoking and aging period. Salt draws moisture from the cells as it penetrates the ham at one inch every seven days. The meat proteins dissolve in salt and water and become tacky. When heated, the dissolved proteins set up and bind the meat, thus preserving it from spoilage or—in lay terms—"curing" it. The salt retards the development of rancidity by inhibiting the growth of bacteria and restricting the action of certain enzymes and micro-organisms. The product that emerges from this process is well-marbled and covered with a clear, firm, fiber-free fat that adds considerably to the flavor.

In colonial Virginia the razorback hogs from which the Virginia hams were cured were let loose to forage in the peanut fields in the fall, thus over the years they developed an oily type flesh which is believed to produce a better ham. Being of an oily nature they do not dry out as hard as a corn-fed hog, which possesses a firm white fat.

With the invention of the combine which picked the peanut vines clean and left little for the hogs, and the increase in demand for hams which the peanut belt could not supply, hogs had to come from other sources to produce Virginia hams.

In the deep south, hogs were turned into soybean fields at harvest time, and thus developed the same oily flesh as those fed peanuts. These are now imported to produce the same fine quality hams.

While Virginia hams are thought to have a special flavor because of the diet of the hogs from which they are cured, other countries share the same belief. The Germans feed the hogs that produce the aged Westphalian a diet of sugar beets, while the Italian hogs whose hinder part is used to prepare the famous Prosciutto are fed chestnuts in some regions, and whey from the local cheese production in the Parma region.

The early settlers slaughtered their hogs during the winter because they had no refrigeration; they aged the hams with summer heat, and served them to their families and guests in the fall. This process took ten to twelve months. Under present conditions the same quality hams may now be cured in less than ninety days. This reduces the curing time and the cost to the consumer because the new process does not tie up the enormous amount of money that is necessary to maintain an inventory of hams for a period of nine to twelve months as in the past.

# THE CURING PROCESS

Curing of hams is the process by which different chemicals are introduced into the meat to prevent spoilage and retain its flavor and color. Hams are cured by two basic techniques: dry cure and wet cure. In the dry cure technique, the ham is rubbed with the dry curing mixture (salt and sodium nitrate) and allowed to stand until the meat is permeated. Salt will only penetrate the meat in the form of liquid brine, and the dry salt forms brine when it comes into contact with the natural juice of the ham. This is a slow method used to cure Prosciutto, Country, and Virginia hams.

Wet cure describes two processes, brine pickle cure and pickle injection cure. Brine pickle cure involves soaking the ham in a brine solution until saturated. In earlier times, the necessary amount of salt was judged by adding salt to the desired amount of water until the solution would float an egg. Westphalian and some forms of tenderized or sugar cured hams are cured in this brine pickle. Pickle injection is the the injecting of salt brine into the hams. Boned and rolled ham, boiled ham, water-added smoked ham, and tenderized or sugar cured hams are cured by this method.

The hams of today are superior to those available a few years ago due to scientific development of the animals and to the modernized, sanitary facilities in which they are produced. The curing process today is federally inspected by the United States Department of Agriculture and adheres to its guidelines and rules for consumer protection.

Each region of the United States has its own variation of the method of curing a Country ham and each, through state or regional pride, thinks it has developed the best curing method. However, passing judgment on this argument is like judging who has the prettiest wife, and has been known to cause dissent among friends, and even add a gloomy note to a festive occasion, as with the following tale.

Horace, Jethro and several other farmers had sat around the black cast iron potbellied stove in Four Corners General Store many brisk windy November evenings trading stories—many of them the fabrications of some vivid imaginations.

Jethro was a robust man, forty pounds overweight for his 5 foot, 10 inch frame, and his stomach hung two inches over his belt; he wore a western hat that had seen many a fall harvest. On the night before Thanksgiving, as on so many other evenings that this group had gathered in the general store, Jethro switched his oversized wad of Brown Mule chewing tobacco from side to side, bragging about the sweet and tasty Country hams he had cured the previous winter, and how well his little lady had said they turned out.

Listening with envy was Horace, a thin-as-a-beanpole man whose red suspenders held his overall pants three inches above his high top shoes. Horace had packed his meat in early January. Two days after the hog killing a freeze had "set in" that lasted two weeks, and the meat had frozen and not taken the salt to the bone properly. Consequently, when he smoked the meat out back over hickory logs in the old weather-beaten smokehouse that had housed the prize hams of his family for a couple of generations, the hams were found to be spoiled and had to be dumped for the creatures of the forest to scavenge.

On Thanksgiving day, following a month of these meetings at the general store, Jethro's little lady had invited cousin Horace's family to dinner as they had done for many previous years, and she had prepared one of Jethro's prize hams for the occasion. Horace was called on to give the Thanksgiving blessing. Inspired by all the evenings of having listened to Jethro brag about his hams, Horace proceeded with the blessing:

Good Lord in Heaven up above
Look down upon this ham.
Send us something fittin' to eat,
For this ain't worth a damn!

These smokehouses which adjoin the Joel E.
Harrell, Sr., farm near Suffolk, Virginia, were
built in 1924. They were among the first ever
to be under federal inspection and were used
to smoke and age up to twenty-four thousand
hams, shoulders, and sides a year. Drawing
by Nat Thompson.

The smokehouse was the center of attraction of the farm buildings, and city dwellers would ride into the country to purchase their meat. These barns and smokehouse are part of the outbuildings at New Towne Haven Plantation in Isle of Wight, the home of Mr. and Mrs. Richard L. Turner.

# PURCHASING A HAM

In buying a ham, you must consider that the cost per serving is lower and the meat content higher than most other forms of meat, even though the unit cost may be higher.

Ham is a very nutritious food. It is an excellent source of protein, the nutrient that is made up of amino acids. These are necessary to build, repair, and maintain healthy body tissues. Ham includes a significant amount of B vitamins which are essential for a good appetite, good mental health, and a healthy skin. These include thiamine, niacin, and riboflavin.

According to the food chart "Nutrients in Common Foods in Terms of Household Measure" published by the United States Department of Agriculture, a three ounce portion of boneless smoked ham contains:

2.5 milligrams IRON
4.6 milligrams THIAMINE
.18 milligrams RIBOFLAVIN
3.5 milligrams NIACIN
20 grams PROTEIN
9 grams CALCIUM
28 grams FAT
39 percent WATER
340 calories

Hams can usually be purchased cheaper on special features during the months of May and September. These two months precede the holiday seasons when demand for ham is the greatest. They can be bought for a discount and saved until you need them for a summer picnic or a holiday dinner.

Be sure to hang a Country ham in a cool dry place until ready for use. Do not lay the ham down flat on a shelf or table, for it will absorb moisture from other substances just like a sponge. Hang the ham in a cool dry place so it will not touch the wall or other hams, and it will keep in good condition as long as desired without refrigeration.

Virginia and Country hams may be covered with mold, a normal characteristic. It is the same type mold found in aged cheeses and like mold on cheeses, it is not harmful. It is formed during the curing process by a reaction of the moisture from the ham with the heat and humidity in the air. *Do not discard* your ham if covered with mold. Simply wash the ham in hot water and scrub off the mold with a stiff vegetable brush.

Many people receive Virginia hams as gifts—the highest compliment a friend could pay you! Unfortunately, many of these prized gifts have been discarded because of lack of knowledge about the mold being a by-product of the aging process.

One young Virginia college student in New York City had befriended some Yankee classmates. To show appreciation of their northern hospitality he sent them a Virginia ham for a Christmas gift. A week later he received a thank you, but also a regret that the ham had to be thrown away because it was covered with mold and obviously no good. He explained much too late, of course, that this mold was a significant part of a very valuable ham, and that he wished he had cooked the ham before mailing it to them!

# COOKING HAM

The first cookbook printed in America was *The Compleat Housewife* by E. Smith. It was reprinted in 1742 in Williamsburg by William Parks, after first having been published in England in 1724. It described the English method of curing hams:

## To Salt and Dry a Ham of Bacon

Take English Bay-Salt, and put it into a Vessel of Water suitable to the quantity of Hams you do; make your Pickle strong enough to bear an Egg with Your Bay-Salt; then boil and scum it very well; then let the Pickle be thoroughly cold, and put into it so much Red-Saunders as will make it the Colour of Claret; then let your Pickle stand three Days before you put your hams into it. The Hams must lie in the Pickle three weeks; then carefully dry them where wood is burnt.

In 1824 Mary Randolph, a close relative of Thomas Jefferson, wrote a cookbook entitled *The Virginia Housewife*. By this time the Americans had become proud of their own curing process, and the allegiance to British tradition had begun to wane. This book, printed eighty-two years after *The Compleat Housewife*, gave only the American method of curing ham, which is similar to that still used today:

Salt hams before they get cold...rub a large tablespoonful of salt petre on the inside of each ham, for some minutes, then rub both sides well with salt, sprinkle the bottoms of the tub with salt, lay the hams with the skin downward, and put a good deal of salt between each layer... When hams have been in salt four weeks, hang them to smoke. If they remain longer on salt they will be hard. Remember to hang the hams and shoulders with the hocks down to preserve the juices. Make a good smoke every morning and be careful not to have a blaze; the smokehouse should stand alone, for any additional heat will spoil the meat.

During the hot weather, beginning the first of April, it should be occasionally taken down, examined, rubbed with hickory ashes, and hung up again.

Ham cookery depends upon the type and cut of ham. Meat packers describe suitable methods of cooking their product on the label, so read it carefully. The methods of cooking are:

**Roasting or Baking:** Place fat side of whole ham or ham piece on rack in roasting pan. Insert meat thermometer. Do not add water; do not cover. Bake at 325° according to *Ham Cooking Chart*. If desired, glaze ham during the last thirty minutes of baking time.

**Whole Country Ham:** If you are baking a Country ham and the ham is very old, soak for 24 hours in water. Scrub ham thoroughly and place in a roaster fat side up. It is necessary to add about 5 cups of water or other liquid, to a depth of about 2 inches in the roaster, then cover. Governor and Mrs. James E. Holshouser, Jr., of North Carolina, recommend the addition of fruit juice, peach or pear pickle juice, cola, cider, or any other flavored liquid your family and guests will like. Roast about 20 minutes per pound, or until ham is tender, basting often. When ham is almost done, remove the rind, trim off the excess fat, score the surface of the fat with diagonal slashes, and glaze. Select a glaze that will complement the flavor of the ham cooking liquid.

**Broiling Ham Slices:** Set oven regulator for broiling. To prevent ham slices from curling during cooking, slice the fat edge of ham about every ¾ inch. Place slice on cold rack of broiler pan. Broil about three inches from heat until meat is brown on one side. Turn ham slice and cook until other side is well browned. Certain glazes or sauces can be brushed on the ham slice during cooking. Cooked ham slices will only need to be heated through, but uncooked slices may need to be turned several times to be thoroughly cooked, depending on the thickness of the slice.

**Panbroiling Ham Slices:** Place slices in a heavy frying pan. Do not add fat or water and do not cover. Cook slowly, letting the ham cook in its own fat. Brown meat on both sides. Country sliced ham will taste less salty if the slice is steamed in about one inch of water for a few minutes before frying; pour off water and let ham fry in its own fat.

**Panfry:** In a heavy skillet fry ham in a small amount of fat. Do not cover. Cook on medium heat, turning the ham occasionally until done.

**New Oven Method:** This method is a convenient, energy-saving way of cooking a 10 to 14 pound tenderized or Country ham. Wash and soak the Country ham overnight. Preheat oven to 500°. Put ham, skin side up, in roaster with all vents closed. Pour in 8 cups of cold water. Cover roaster tightly. Place in preheated oven and let cook at 500° for 15 minutes. *Do not open* oven door. Turn oven off for 3 hours. It is important to time accurately. After 3 hours, turn oven back on for 15 minutes. Turn oven off, and let ham remain in oven for about 8 hours. Remove from oven and skin ham. Rub with brown sugar and stud with cloves. Bake about 30 minutes until brown. Cool and slice thin. It's great! For a different flavor, try 8 cups of ginger ale or apple juice or cider instead of water.

**Kettle Method:** This method is suitable for cooking a whole or half air-dried or smoked Country ham as well as Smithfield or Virginia ham. Select a pot or ham boiler large enough to hold the ham when completely immersed in water. An expensive ham boiler or pot is not necessary. The old-fashioned blue and white enamel pots are just as good for this as the modern stainless steel ones, and can be purchased at a much lower price. It will be worth the investment because cooking in it one time will more than pay for itself when comparing the cost of an un-cooked versus a pre-cooked ham. When the ham is completely covered with water, bring the water to a boil, then reduce the heat, simmer and cook slowly, covered, until done, according to cooking chart. The meat separating from the bone on the butt end is an indication that it is done. Soak any ham over six months old for at least 12 to 24 hours before cooking if you prefer a less salty taste.

**Grilling:** For charcoal grilling, start your fire about 30 minutes before the ham steak or slices are to be grilled. Lining the grill with heavy aluminum foil will make for easier cleaning and will reflect the heat. With lighting fluid, soak the charcoal briquets which have been stacked in the bottom of the grill in the shape of a pyramid. Let them stand about one minute before lighting. When the burning charcoal turns grayish-white, spread the coals evenly over the bottom of the grill. Place the ham steaks or slices on the grill. Ham steaks can be basted with a favorite sauce for additional flavor. Popular Country ham breakfast slices and smoked sugar-cured slices make delicious appetizers when charcoaled for about 4 to 5 minutes per side. Slice the ham in bite size pieces and serve at once. This is a delicious hors d'oeuvre treat for a picnic.

**Microwave Method:** This method for cooking a ham in a microwave oven was tested in a Litton. Each brand has its own idiosyncrasies, and you will need to adapt the settings to your own microwave oven.

Place, fat side up, in a glass dish that is at least two inches deep:

**1 half ham, 7 to 8 pounds**

Add:

**1 inch water**

Cover with clear plastic wrap. Cook 10 minutes on HIGH. Uncover, turn fat side down, re-cover, and cook 10 more minutes on HIGH. Uncover, turn fat side back up, re-cover, and cook 10 more minutes on HIGH. Insert meat thermometer that comes with oven. Set the dial at 155°. Cook for 30 minutes on ROAST until the desired temperature of 155° is reached. Remove ham from oven to a platter. Wrap ham in aluminum foil for 15 minutes. Test for doneness because the ham continues to cook while wrapped in foil. Leave wrapped longer if necessary. Slice and serve.

# Ham Cooking Chart

| Type Of Ham | Cut | Approx. Wt. Lbs. | Method Of Cooking | Top Of Range Or Oven Temp. | Approx. Cooking Time Minutes Per Lb. | Approx. Total Cooking Time Hours | Meat Thermometer Reading On Removal From Oven | Remarks |
|---|---|---|---|---|---|---|---|---|
| Fresh | Whole | 10-14 | In liquid | Simmer 190 | 20-24 | 3½-4 | 180 | ¼-½ cup vinegar added to water will reduce fresh pork taste |
| | Whole | 10-14 | Baking | 325 | 20-24 | 3½-4 | | |
| | Half | | In liquid | Simmer 190 | 35-40 | 2¾-4 | | |
| | Half | 5-8 | Baking | 325 | 35-40 | 2¾-4 | 180 | |
| Corned Dry | Whole | 10-14 | In liquid | Simmer 190 | 25 | 4-4½ | 170 | Soak before cooking |
| | Whole | | Bake | 325 | 25 | 4-4½ | | |
| Corned Wet | Whole | 10-14 | In liquid | Simmer 190 | 25 | 4-4½ | 180 | Soak before cooking |
| | Whole | | Bake | 325 | 25 | 4-4½ | | |
| Smoked or Sugar Cured or Tender-ized or Packers or Cook-Before Eating | Whole | 10-14 | Bake | 325 | 18-20 | 3-4 1/3 | 160 | |
| | Slice | 3-4 ounces | Fry | Medium | 5-6 | | | |
| | Shank Half | 3-4 | Bake | 325 | 35-40 | 1¾-2 2/3 | 160 | |
| | Butt Half | 3-4 | Bake | 325 | 35-40 | 1¾-2 2/3 | 160 | |
| Fully Cooked | Whole | 10-14 | Bake | 325 | 15 | 2½-3½ | 135 | These instructions describe length of time to heat ham including addition of glazes or sauces |
| Smoked Tender-ized | Slice Half Bone-less | 3-4 ounces 4-5 | Fry Bake | Medium 325 | 15 | 3-4 min. 1-2 | 135 | |
| Sugar Cured | Half Bone-less | 4-5 | Bake | 325 | 15 | 1-2 | 135 | |
| Packers | Whole Bone-less | 8-10 | Bake | 325 | 15 | 2-2¼ | 135 | |

| Type Of Ham | Cut | Approx. Wt. Lbs. | Method Of Cooking | Top Of Range Oven Temp. | Approx. Cooking Time Minutes Per Lb. | Approx. Total Cooking Time Hours | Meat Thermometer Reading On Removal From Oven | Remarks |
|---|---|---|---|---|---|---|---|---|
| Boned and Rolled are Fully Cooked | Slice 3/8" | 3-4 ounces | Fry | Medium | 3-4 min. on each side | | | |
| | | | Broil | | | | | |
| Westphalia | Shoulder Butt | 4-6 | Bake | 325 | 20 | 1½-2 | | |
| Prosciutto | | Needs | No Cooking | — | Eat As | Is | | |
| Smoked Country Ham | Whole | 10-14 | In liquid | Simmer 190 | 20 | 3½-4¾ | 190 | Soak 12-24 hours before cooking |
| | Whole | 10-14 | Bake | 325 | 20 | 3½-4¾ | 190 | |
| | Half | 5-8 | In liquid | Simmer 190 | 35 | 2¾-4¾ | | A visual guide is that when meat begins to separate from bone or end of ham, it is done |
| | | | Bake | 325 | 35 | 2¾-4¾ | 190 | |
| | Slice | 1/8" thick | Fry | Medium | | 8-10 min. | | Cover with water and steam for less salty taste |
| | Slice | 3/4" thick | Broil | | | 10-12 min. | | |
| Air Dried Country Ham Non-Smoked | Whole | 10-14 | In liquid | Simmer 190 | 20 | 4-5 | | Soak 12-24 hours for less salty taste |
| | Whole | 10-14 | Bake | 325 | 20 | 4-5 | | |
| | Half | 5-8 | In liquid | Simmer 190 | 35 | 3½-4¾ | | |
| | | | Bake | 325 | 35 | 3½-4¾ | | |
| | Slice | 1/8" thick | Fry | Medium | 35-40 | 8-10 min. | | Cover with water and steam for less salty taste |
| | Slice | 3/4" thick | Broil | | | 10-12 min. | | |
| Smithfield or Virginia | Whole | 10-14 | In liquid | Simmer 190 | 25 | 5-5½ | | Soak for 24 hours before cooking for less salty flavor. Cook covered with water. All hams over 6 months in age should definitely be cooked in liquid. |

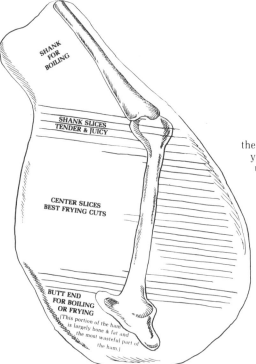

SHANK
FOR
BOILING

SHANK SLICES
TENDER & JUICY

CENTER SLICES
BEST FRYING CUTS

BUTT END
FOR BOILING
OR FRYING
[This portion of the ham
is largely bone & fat and
the most wasteful part of
the ham.]

This diagram shows which parts of the ham can be used to your advantage if you prefer to fry the best portions and use the rest for seasoning vegetables or making ham soups.

The sections designated as center slices for frying may also be left whole and baked, for this section gives the best full slices and has only one bone that is easily removed after cooking.

Cut a wedge-shaped piece from the ham, about 6 inches in from end of hock. Slice thin at 45° angle, bringing knife to bone. As slices become larger, slightly decrease angle of knife for equal-sized servings.

# SLICING, CARVING, AND SERVING

In order to best utilize all of the succulent meat on a ham, you should bone the ham while it is hot. This allows the meat to detach from the bone rather easily, leaving only enough meat on the bone to make one of our hambone soups that are so great for lunch on a nippy day.

The ham is easier to slice without the bone; however, you will get more servings by slicing on a meat slicer, if available. Allow the ham to cool completely for easy slicing.

To bone cooked ham, allow to cool just until you can handle it with the aid of kitchen gloves. Follow the steps in these diagrams for boning and slicing.

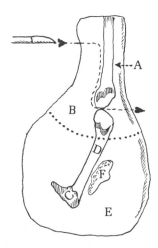

**Bone as Follows:**

A. Remove part of shank
    with bone in.
B. Remove skin.
C. Remove aitch bone.
D. Remove femur.
E. Defat ham.
F. Remove seam fat.

## SERVING TABLE

Country ham should be sliced paper thin for ham biscuits and a little thicker for dinner. Smoked ham can be sliced a little thicker for dinner.

| Size in Pounds | Number Slices | Ham Alone Will Serve the Following for Dinner | Ham & Another Meat Will Serve the Following for Dinner | Ham Biscuits Will Make the Following Number |
|---|---|---|---|---|
| 10 | 64 | 25 | 38 | 250 |
| 12 | 76 | 30 | 45 | 300 |
| 14 | 88 | 35 | 52 | 350 |
| 16 | 100 | 42 | 60 | 400 |

# PART II
# HAMMING IT UP

Country breads and fresh vegetables grace this early eighteenth century fireplace and hearth, located on Windsor Castle farm in Smithfield in Isle of Wight County, Virginia. After lengthy research and careful planning, the present owners, Mr. and Mrs. Charles Samuel Betts, Jr., restored the old kitchen to its authentic 1700s charm.

Windsor Castle is the original land grant name and was so called, as the story goes, because the original bricks came from England. The farm originally belonged to Arthur Smith, the founder of Smithfield.

# COUNTRY COOKING

The term country cooking describes old-fashioned down home cooking where everything was made from scratch by people who relied on the meat and produce grown on the farm to feed their families the year around. Food was preserved by canning, drying, or smoking. Many quarts of vegetables and fruits were "put-up" in the late summer and early autumn when the crops and gardens were harvested. Peaches, plums, apples, and other fruits were spread out on clean cloth strips to dry. Cabbages were placed in barrels in a brine solution to make sauerkraut, particularly popular among settlers of German descent.

Hog killings were a ceremonial occasion looked forward to by young and old. It was indeed a family day; everyone had a chore. Often small farm owners would get together and bring their hogs to one central farm for a joint venture of "killing and fixing." By helping each other they saved on the cost of additional labor.

A cold day was always picked for hog killing, as it was necessary that the temperature be below 45 degrees Fahrenheit in order to remove the body heat from the carcass.

The huge black caldron was filled with water and placed over an open fire in order to start boiling. Getting the fire going in the early dawn and filling the caldron was usually the responsibility of one of the boys in the family. A blow from an ax handle stunned the animal before it was slit for "bleeding," or it was shot. This was accepted as a matter of necessity and not considered gruesome. The hair was then scraped away with a sharp knife and boiling water. For cutting, the carcass was then hung and stretched on a wooden gambol stick.

After the hogs were slaughtered and dressed, many good country pork products were made. Some of these were liver pudding, souse, fresh scrapple, sausage and dan doodle (a sausage stuffed in a casing and smoked). The sweetbreads or pancreas glands were considered a delicacy even then. They were dipped in batter and fried.

To preserve fresh sausage, the housewife would pat the sausage into cakes and fry them. These cakes were then packed into quart jars or stone crocks and covered with the grease left from frying. This sealed the containers, keeping them air tight. Tenderloin and pork chops were also fried, packed in containers, and covered with the remaining grease to seal out the air and preserve the meat. Spareribs and backbones were used right away. The hams, shoulders, and sides were "salted down."

Some of the farmers would smoke their hams. In Tidewater, smoking meat was very popular; however, in the mountain regions of Virginia, after the salting stage, a string was tied around the hocks and the hams were bagged then hung to dry and age without smoking. The pig's feet were cleaned, cooked, and stored in jars filled with vinegar to preserve them... the result: pickled pig's feet.

Every part of the hog was used except the hair. Today, however, hog hair is pressed and used in the making of men's felt hats among other things. Even the bladder had merit! Grandfather Roberson recalled that the youngsters would often clamor for it because after it was cleaned they would insert a reed in one end and blow it up like a balloon. This pro-

vided hours of fun as modern-day balloons did not exist. Some of the fat was cooked down to make lard. The particles of skin and fat which remained after the fat was rendered were called cracklings. These floated to the top of the grease and were skimmed off and saved to make cracklin' bread. Rolled into a biscuit dough, they made cracklin' biscuits. Cracklings were put into airtight containers and kept through the winter in a cool place. These cracklings were often eaten as snacks, as we would eat potato chips today. Several days after the "killing," soap was made by cooking the remaining fat from the hog with lye in the large black caldron over an outdoor open fire. The lye soap was used for washing dishes and clothes, not for bathing.

The eighteenth and nineteenth century housewife was often responsible for feeding the farm hands as well as her own family. Even if she had cooks to help with this chore, she did not have today's conveniences. The old cast iron wood-burning stove was the hub of much of the household activity; on this stove the meals were prepared and heat was generated to warm the kitchen and usually the dining room. Fires were rekindled before dawn to "knock off" the chill of the night as well as to cook the morning meal, which was served around five-thirty or six since the men needed to be in the fields by daybreak. One gentleman reminisced that as a young lad he slept upstairs where it was so cold during the night, that the first thing he would do in the chill of the morning was to run downstairs in his stocking feet, pull a chair in front of the rumbling old cook stove with its opened oven door and warm himself. Bricks were often warmed in the stove and placed in the buggy to keep the children's feet warm during the ride to school.

After breakfast, the next chore was to gather the vegetables from the garden and start the preparation for the midday dinner. It was a true dinner, greatly needed after a morning of hard work. Food was placed in large cooking pots on the back of the stove and allowed to cook slowly until the noon hour. The housewife would then clean and straighten her home while the dinner was simmering. She would, however, stop long enough ahead to mix up a batch of fresh bread. Either corn bread, corn pones, crackling bread, or biscuits were made, and rolls were usually prepared for a Sunday treat. Corn pones are a very heavy corn bread made only of salt, meal and water, baked in the oven.

The popular yard dinner bell would ring to announce the awaiting meal. The bell was also used in emergencies as a warning or to call for help. If a child suddenly got sick, chances are the horse that was needed to take him to the doctor would be in the field working. Some folks kept a buggy horse, but the average farm family could not afford another horse to feed.

The farm hands were greeted by a simmering pot of fresh vegetables and the aroma of hot bread. Ham or pork of some kind and another meat were generally served. They ate in the kitchen, on the back porch, and, during the summer, under the foliage of the large trees that usually surrounded country homes. Quite often hired hands would come to help with the harvest and the curing of meat, not for the money alone, but to feast on these midday dinners.

The food left from lunch would be placed in warming ovens located over the top of the cast iron stove, or a clean cloth would be spread over the food left on the table to await the evening meal.

This cast iron stove and large open kettle, often referred to as the ham boiler, were used to cook the delicious Virginia ham. This large pot method of cooking a ham, we refer to as the "Kettle Method." Grandmother Harrell, Mrs. Joel E. Harrell, Sr., née Cora Parker and known as "Cousin Cora" by her many friends, always used this method. Her outstanding cooking was appreciated and enjoyed by the entire Liberty Spring community. She usually entertained twenty to thirty guests who descended upon her home for dinner on Sunday following church.

The pot liquor the ham was cooked in was cooled and the grease carefully skimmed off the top and stored in a cool place for future seasoning. No part of the ham was ever wasted. The bone was always saved for hearty soups and the meat left on the bone was removed and ground for a delicious ham salad. Even the skin was cut in small pieces and fed to the dogs.

Today many people are restricted against the use of fat in seasoning vegetables. Ham broth that has had the grease removed is perfect for giving that country flavor without the excess fat. A helpful hint is to freeze the ham broth in ice cube trays and then store in plastic bags in the freezer. When ready to use, just pop the cubes in a pot of vegetables for a tasty ham flavor.

For that full "country flavor," greens and cabbage are kept covered with water during the cooking process. However, if you are nutrition conscious, add just enough water or ham broth to keep them from sticking and steam the greens about 20 minutes, or until tender. Season to taste. The steaming method will help preserve the vitamin content and also prevent the breaking down of the celluloid fiber that gives the much needed roughage and bulk to our diet.

Ginger Woo, a Northern mother who had moved South and indoctrinated her family to Southern cooking, which includes seasoning vegetables with country meats, was given a new steamer one Christmas and proceeded to cook her vegetables in it without the familiar seasoning meat. Her family, however, was so upset that she was inspired to compose the following lyric to explain her dilemma.

Vitamins are the thing we hear about
    today
So when I got a steamer for Christmas,
    I decided I would cook my vegetables
    the Northern way.
The first night I tried them no one would
    eat
They said, "This is not the usual food.
Where is the Meat?"
I tried to tell them this was the best way;
It was nutritious.
This was what they had to say:
    "Please Mom, forget the nutrition, add
      the onions and the ham
    That's the way we like them—and the
      vitamins be damn!"

Country cooking was usually a dash of this, a pinch of that, and a handful of lots of good things—or as my friend George Birdsong says, "Why, a recipe is just combining a lot of good foods that go together, anyway." However, I have attempted to describe, after careful collaboration with several excellent country cooks, recipes that reflect the best of Tidewater Virginia country cooking.

## GRANDMOTHER HARRELL'S RECIPE FOR COOKING A WHOLE AGED VIRGINIA HAM "KETTLE METHOD"

Wash thoroughly in warm water:

**Virginia ham**

Soak overnight in cold water. Place a large pot or ham boiler on stove with sufficient water to *cover* ham. When water comes to a boiling point, place ham in pot with skin side up. Place lid on pot. Reduce heat and simmer ham about 20 to 25 minutes per pound until tender (the protruding bone on the back side will separate from the meat). Remove ham from pot. Before it cools, remove skin. Place ham in a baking pan, fat side up. Add:

**1 cup water**

Rub ham with:

**white sugar**

Stick in fat at intervals:

**whole cloves**

Bake until brown in a slow oven (300°) about 30 minutes. Cool the pot liquor the ham was cooked in, skim off the grease, and refrigerate the ham grease for future seasoning. Cook cabbage in remaining ham broth.

# SOUTHERN MARYLAND STUFFED COUNTRY HAM

This is a traditional dish that has been prepared by this method in southern Maryland for at least two hundred years.

Remove muslin bag, and save it. Soak overnight:

**1 ten to twelve pound Country ham**

Drain and simmer by the "Kettle Method" for 1 hour. Let ham cool in the pot liquor. Remove ham, cut off the rind and most of the fat. Bring the liquor in the pot to boiling and drop in:

**3 heads cabbage, chopped**
**2 pounds kale**
**1 pound mustard greens**
**6 or 8 green onions including tops, chopped fine**

You may combine your favorite greens. Cook five minutes, then add seasonings:

**1 tablespoon red pepper**
**1 tablespoon black pepper**
**1 tablespoon dry mustard**
**⅛ teaspoon granulated garlic**
**1 tablespoon celery seed**

When greens are tender, drain thoroughly and chop fine. When ham is cool enough, with a sharp knife, make six to eight vertical slits or incisions about 2 inches apart and 3 inches long. Turn ham over and do the same on the bottom. Stuff the openings or pockets tightly with the greens. Stuff the ham back into the muslin bag. Sew tightly in place in order to keep the stuffing in the pockets. Place ham back in the pot liquor and simmer for at least 2½ more hours or until ham is tender when pierced with a fork. Allow ham to cool in pot. Transfer ham to a large platter without removing the cloth bag. Refrigerate for a few hours before serving. Unwrap ham and slice paper thin. Allow 20 minutes to the pound for total cooking time.

# AUNT EMILY'S HAM FLAVORED BUTTERBEANS

4 to 6 servings

Wash:

**1 quart shelled butterbeans**

Making sure beans are covered, place in pot with:

**1 quart water**

Add for seasoning:

**about ½ pound uncooked country ham or 6 tablespoons ham fat or about 1 tablespoon ham grease or ½ cup cooked ham scraps or 1 ham hock.**

Bring water to boil, reduce heat to low and cook about 1 hour until done—add salt, if needed, If you use a ham hock for flavoring, place it in unsalted water and simmer at least one hour before adding butter beans.

# CORN AND BUTTERBEANS COOKED TOGETHER

10 to 12 servings

Refer to *Aunt Emily's Ham Flavored Butterbeans* recipe. Fifteen minutes before beans are done, add corn cut from 5 ears to each quart of shelled butterbeans. Cook approximately 15 more minutes.

# DRIED BABY LIMAS AND HAM HOCKS

4 servings

Soak for several hours or overnight:

**1 pound dried baby limas**

While limas are soaking, bring to boil:

**2 quarts water**

Add:

**2 ham hocks**

Reduce heat and simmer for 1 hour. Rinse limas; add to ham hock broth and simmer for about 2 hours until they are tender.

# HAM FLAVORED SNAPS OR STRING BEANS

8 to 10 servings

Wash and drop into slightly salted water to cover:

**2 pounds string beans**
**1 small peeled onion (optional)**

Add:

**4 tablespoons ham grease or**
**1/3 cup ham fat or 1 cup chopped ham scraps or 1 ham hock**

Cook for 1 hour until tender. Check beans during cooking time to make sure the vegetables remain covered with water. If you cannot eat ham fat, cook snaps in ham *broth* after the fat has been skimmed off the top. If you use a ham hock, bring unsalted water to a boil and simmer at least 1 hour before adding beans. You can add white potatoes at the same time for an additional vegetable.

# HAM FLAVORED CABBAGE

4 servings

Grandmother Harrell always cooked cabbage or some type of greens the same day as the ham so that full advantage could be taken of the ham broth.

Wash and chop:

**1 large head cabbage**

Drop into boiling, degreased:

**ham broth**

Cook until tender, approximately 15 to 30 minutes. No salt will be required because of the salty broth.

If *Broth* is not available, bring to a boil:

**1 cup water**

Add chopped cabbage and:

**¼ cup ham scraps or ham fat**

Cook until tender. Add salt, if necessary.

# HAM HOCKS 'N' CABBAGE DINNER

6 servings

Put in a pot:

**2 quarts water**
**3 ham hocks**

Bring to boil and reduce heat to simmer; cook about 2 hours. Remove hocks, wrap in foil to keep warm. Put

in pot with this ham broth and cook for about 20 minutes:

**2 heads cabbage, quartered**
**6 Irish potatoes, peeled**

Place cabbage and potatoes on serving platter; slice meat from ham hocks and serve with the vegetables.

# HATTIE'S COLLARDS

4 to 6 servings

Ham hocks and greens are truly examples of country cooking, known to some folks as "soul food." The term "greens" includes mustard, turnip, collards, hanover, and kale. Collards freeze well raw or cooked.

Bring to a boil:

**2½ quarts water**
**1 ham hock**

Reduce heat and simmer 1½ hours or until tender. Meanwhile, wash thoroughly:

**1½ pounds collards**

Remove stems and wash again. Add

to tender ham hock broth and cook about 1½ hours or until done. Season to taste and serve. All greens may be cooked by this method.

If ham hock is not available, simmer greens 1½ hours in:

**2½ quarts ham broth**

If *Ham Broth* is unavailable, simmer greens 1½ hours in:

**2½ quarts water**

For the last 20 minutes of cooking time, add:

**2 tablespoons ham grease**

---

## BLACK EYED PEAS WITH HAM HOCKS

6 to 8 servings

Wash thoroughly and pick over:

**1 pound black eyed peas**

Place peas in saucepan and add:

    **2 quarts water**
    **1 ham hock or**
      **2 tablespoons ham grease or**
      **4 tablespoons diced ham fat**
**dash salt**

**1 pod red hot pepper (optional)**
**2 medium onions, quartered (optional)**

Cover, bring to a boil, reduce heat and simmer until peas and ham hock are tender. If water boils down, add more hot water to keep peas covered. If you want the meat from the ham hocks for supper, use 2 hocks.

---

## GARDEN PEAS

8 servings

Shell and wash:

    **1 quart of shelled garden peas**

Put in about 1 quart of slightly salted water, making sure peas are covered. Add:

    **2 tablespoons ham grease or**
      **4 tablespoons ham fat or 1 slice**

    **uncooked ham or 1 ham hock**

Bring water to boil, reduce heat to low and simmer about 1 hour. If you use a ham hock, bring unsalted water to a boil and simmer hock for 1 hour, or until meat leaves the bone. Remove hock, wrap in foil to keep warm. Add peas and cook until tender. Season to taste.

# HAM AND CYMBLING CASSEROLE

6 servings

Cymblings are a type of squash. They are known in the North as white squash. The colloquial term, however, is "cymlin'." I first tasted this dressed up version of cymlin's at the Chuckatuck home of Carol Godwin Frohman; her cooking talents range from country to gourmet. When I requested the recipe she replied that this was just an old-fashioned country dish that men really enjoyed and it got better each day it was kept.
Scrub and cut in medium size pieces:

**10 medium cymblings**

Boil in a small amount of slightly salted water, barely covering cymblings, until soft. Fry until crisp and drain on paper towels:

**4 slices bacon**

In remaining drippings, fry until golden brown or translucent:

**2 large onions, chopped**

Drain squash, mash, and add to skillet with onions. Sprinkle with:

**salt and pepper**
**dash Tabasco (optional)**

Cook slowly about 1 to 1½ hours until liquid is gone, stirring occasionally. You can serve the cymblings at this point or continue for the extra special full flavor. Pour into a greased flat casserole, 2 inches in depth. Mix and sprinkle over casserole:

**1 cup chopped cooked ham**
**1 cup grated Cheddar cheese**
**crumbled bacon**

Bake at 325° for 15 to 20 minutes until cheese melts.

You can also alternate layers of squash, ham, and cheese. Repeat process. If cymblings are not available, use yellow-necked squash. If you have a few yellow-necked squash and a few cymblings, combine them.

# FRIED TENNESSEE COUNTRY HAM WITH RED EYE GRAVY

1 serving

Betty Blanton, wife of Ray Blanton, Governor of Tennessee, enjoys this traditional Southern recipe as one of her favorite dishes. In the South some folks say that the fragrance of ham frying is enough to make a body be dissatisfied with anything else that might be served him. In Virginia we serve it for breakfast with grits and hot biscuits. Water may be used in place of the coffee.

Trim off skin and fry quickly in an ungreased hot skillet, selecting one aged at least 18 months and preferably 2 years:

**¼ inch thick center cut Country ham slice**

Remove ham to hot platter. To pan drippings add:

**4 tablespoons black coffee**

Pour over ham and serve.

# TIDEWATER BOILED DINNER

4 servings

This is a hearty autumn meal. Serve with *Mamie's Old Fashioned Skillet Cornbread* and a congealed salad.

Bring to a boil:

**2 quarts water**

Add and simmer until tender, about 2 hours:

**2 ham hocks**

Remove hocks from water and wrap in foil. In the same ham stock, cook for 15 minutes:

**8 medium potatoes, peeled**
**8 to 9 carrots, peeled and cut in half**

Chop and add to same pot and cook for 20 minutes:

**1 large head cabbage**

Remove vegetables to serving plates and top with pieces of ham from the hock.

# OYSTER-HAM DRESSING

6 to 8 servings

This dressing is delicious with turkey.

Preheat oven to 325°. In a saucepan, melt:

**1 stick butter or margarine**

Add and sauté until almost done:

**1 stalk celery, chopped**
**1 large onion, diced**
**4 tablespoons chopped parsley**

Sprinkle with:

**salt and pepper**

In a large bowl combine the above mixture with:

**1 package stuffing mix or 4 cups homemade bread stuffing**
**1 pint to 1 quart oysters, cut in thirds**
**1 cup chopped cooked Country ham**

Mix well, then pour into a greased baking dish. Make sure the dressing is moist when put in the oven. Bake for 20 minutes.

# COUNTRY HAM PIE

6 to 8 servings

Dr. Dorothy Rowe, head of the home economics department at Madison College, describes her favorite ham recipe as "country cooking" because her family often made this on the farm. It is a good way to use those less than perfect pieces of ham, and you can vary the dish to suit your taste as does any good country cook. A ready to use biscuit dough is great for a quick top!

Peel and slice ¼ inch thick:

**6 potatoes**
**1 onion**

Cook potatoes and onions until tender with:

**1 slice cooked Country ham, chopped or 1 cup chopped**

**cooked ham**
**2 cups water**

Thicken the broth with:

**2 tablespoons flour**

Pour into a deep baking dish or pan. Top with:

**biscuit dough**

Bake at 425° for 12 minutes or until nicely brown.

---

## STEWED POTATOES AND HAM

4 to 6 servings

Place in pot:

**1 quart water**
**1 medium onion, sliced**
**1 cup minced ham or**
    **bits with a little fat left on or**

**1 ham bone**
**6 medium potatoes, chopped**

Bring to a boil, reduce heat and cook for about 20 minutes until potatoes are tender.

---

## RED BEANS AND RICE

6 to 8 servings

This is a typical creole dish. The beans are special, but it is not the soaking that makes them that way. The secret is the cracked hambone.

Soak overnight or at least 5 to 6 hours:

**2 cups dried red kidney beans**

In a large saucepan place:

**1 hambone, cracked**
**2 quarts water**

Bring to a boil and simmer for 20 to 30 minutes. Drain water off beans and add beans to ham stock. The stock should cover the beans by at least three inches; if not add more water. Sauté:

**2 tablespoons olive oil**
**¼ cup chopped onion**
**1 tablespoon parsley**
**2 stalks celery including leaves, chopped**

Add to the bean pot and simmer for about three hours or until soft and creamy. Serve over rice. Pass olive oil and vinegar.

# BREADS

Many country breads are derivatives of Indian maize bread made from crushed corn. The settlers copied the Indians in the use of this newly discovered vegetable. The word cornpone probably comes from the Indian word *appone*.

Cornpone, *Corn Meal Dodgers* or dumplings, fried cornbread, and hush puppies are country cousins. They are made from meal mixed into a dough with cold water and salt in proportion to the quantities to be made; the real country cook makes these to perfection and is never known to measure. Cornpone, *Corn Meal Dodgers*, or dumplings and hush puppies are all shaped into oval mounds; it is traditional to leave the imprint of two or four fingers on top of the dodgers or cornpone, a kind of cook's trademark, before baking.

## CORN MEAL DODGERS

Makes 8

These are cooked in the pot liquor from collards, sallet, kale, cabbage or other greens.

Place in a bowl:

**1 cup corn meal**
**½ teaspoon salt**

Add enough to form a moist batter that can be handled in the hand:

**about 2 tablespoons water**

Shape into flat cakes about ¼ inch thick and two inches in diameter. Drop into the boiling pot liquor. Cook until done, about 10 minutes. The texture will be soft, but firm enough to hold together.

## FRIED CORNBREAD

Makes 6 to 8

Mix in a small bowl:

**1 cup corn meal**
**2 tablespoons self-rising flour**
**pinch salt**

Mix in enough until batter is the consistency of pancake batter:

**water**

Drop by tablespoons into a hot pan containing about:

**⅛ inch cooking oil or**
**ham drippings**

Brown on one side then on the other.

# FRIED CORN MEAL FRITTERS

Makes 6 to 8

In a small bowl combine:

**1 cup corn meal**
**½ cup all purpose flour**
**pinch salt**
**pinch baking powder**

Add enough to make a sticky but not-too stiff batter:

**1 tablespoon each (approx.) of milk and water**

Drop by tablespoons into a heated pan containing:

**⅛ inch oil or shortening or ham drippings**

Fry on one side until brown; turn.

# CORN STICKS

Makes 12 to 14

Preheat oven to 425°. Sift together:

**1 cup corn meal**
**1 cup flour**
**2 tablespoons sugar**
**½ teaspoon salt**
**3 teaspoons baking powder**

Add:

**1 egg**
**1 cup milk**
**¼ cup melted shortening**

Beat until smooth; do not overbeat. Pour batter in well greased, heated cornstick irons. Bake for 15 minutes.

# LACY CORN CAKES

Makes 36

Beat until light:

**2 eggs**

Add:

**2 cups milk**

Slowly add:

**1 cup plus 5 tablespoons corn meal**

**1 teaspoon salt**

Mix well and add:

**4 tablespoons melted butter or margarine**

Drop by spoonfuls onto a hot well-greased griddle. Stir batter each time a spoonful is removed. Brown on one side, then the other. These cakes are paper thin.

# MAMIE'S OLD-FASHIONED SKILLET CORN BREAD

6 servings

Pouring the batter into a hot skillet is the secret of a rich golden crust!

Preheat oven to 425°. Sift together into a mixing bowl:

**2 cups corn meal**
**1 cup flour**
**1 teaspoon baking powder**
**½ teaspoon salt**

Beat in:

**2 cups buttermilk**
**1 egg**
**2 tablespoons mayonnaise**

Stir until well blended. You may need to add more milk to thin the batter. Pour into a hot, generously greased iron skillet. Bake for about 25 minutes or until nicely browned.

# OLD-FASHIONED SPOON BREAD

4 to 6 servings

Connie Bunch, my faithful typist, gave me her old-fashioned spoon bread recipe. It is delicious with fresh vegetables seasoned with ham stock. Serve hot with lots of butter.

Into mixing bowl put:

**1 cup water ground corn meal**
**2 cups boiling water**

Mix well, then add:

**1 cup milk**
**2 eggs, beaten**
**3 tablespoons melted butter**
**3 tablespoons sugar**
**½ teaspoon salt**

Fold in lightly:

**2 tablespoons baking powder**

Pour into a greased baking dish or 2 quart casserole dish. Bake in a 450° oven until top is golden brown, about 25 to 30 minutes.

# MEXICAN SPOON BREAD

8 servings

This is delicious served with sliced ham.

Preheat oven to 400°.

*Step One:* Mix the following ingredients:

**1 pound can cream style corn**
**¾ cup milk**
**5 tablespoons plus 1 teaspoon salad oil**

2 eggs
1 cup yellow corn meal
½ teaspoon soda
1 teaspoon salt

*Step Two:* Pour half of the batter in a well greased 9 by 9 inch baking dish. Spread with:

½ four ounce can green chili peppers

¾ cup grated Cheddar cheese

*Step Three:* Spread remaining batter on top and sprinkle with:

½ four ounce can green chili peppers
¾ cup grated Cheddar cheese

Bake for 45 minutes. For a variation omit the salt and add ½ cup finely chopped ham.

# SALLY LUNN

Makes 1 or 2 loaves

*Sally Lunn* is a light and crumbly bread that Southerners have enjoyed and boasted about since colonial times. Its origin is of course English, and many legends describe how it got its name. One such tale is about an eighteenth century English girl named Sally Lunn who baked and sold her golden buns to the gentry on the streets of Bath. Another account portrays an English girl who shouted "soleil et lune" to advertise her buns while walking the streets. The French "soleil et lune" means "sun and moon," and so were the images of these golden buns: rich brown on top and white on bottom. The colonists baked their popular *Sally Lunn* bread in a Turk's head mold, and the traditional recipe has been passed down from one generation to the next. This is Mother's version.

Scald:

2 cups milk

Pour milk over:

½ cup sugar
2 teaspoons salt
½ cup plus 2 tablespoons shortening

Stir until dissolved. Cool to lukewarm. Stir in:

2 packages yeast
3 eggs, beaten until very light

Stir and beat vigorously after each cup is added:

6 cups flour

Beat until smooth. Cover and let rise until double in bulk, about 1 hour. Stir down batter and place in well greased tube pans or bundt pans or two loaf pans. Cover and let rise again until doubled, about 1 hour. If you prefer rolls or buns, grease a muffin tin and shape into balls and place in muffin tins. Bake in a 350° oven for about 30 minutes. Turn out on a rack and cool slightly. Serve warm with butter.

# GRANDMA PREECE'S BUTTERMILK BISCUITS

Makes about 20

Biscuits are the first and most important bread when it comes to serving Virginia ham. Place a thin sliver of ham between a hot buttered biscuit for a heavenly treat. Cut the biscuits cocktail size for your next party.

*Step One:* Preheat oven to 450°. In a mixing bowl, combine:

**2 cups sifted flour**
**3 teaspoons baking powder**
**½ teaspoon salt**
**¼ teaspoon soda**

Stir with a fork. Add:

**¼ cup shortening**
**¾ cup buttermilk**

*Step Two:* Stir until a sticky dough forms. Turn out onto a lightly floured surface; flour on wax paper works nicely. Knead, working in a little flour until dough is not sticky.

*Step Three:* Roll out dough to ¼ inch thickness. Cut out biscuits and place on an ungreased cookie sheet. Brush with melted butter. Bake about 15 minutes or until golden brown.

# LINDSAY'S ALABAMA BISCUITS

Makes 48

If you have never tried a yeast biscuit, you will find these delicious.

*Step One:* Preheat oven to 375°. Sift together:

**2½ cups flour**
**½ teaspoon soda**
**½ teaspoon salt**
**4 tablespoons sugar**

*Step Two:* Dissolve:

**1 yeast cake or 1 package dry yeast**

**1 cup warm buttermilk**

Cut into dry ingredients:

**6 tablespoons shortening**

Add the milk mixture. Mix well before turning onto lightly floured surface.

*Step Three:* Knead 30 times. Roll out the dough to ¼ inch thickness. Cut out biscuits with a 1¾ inch round cutter. Dip each piece in:

**melted butter**

Stack in twos. Place in a warm place to rise for 2 hours. Bake 15 minutes.

# VIRGINIA GROUND-HAM BISCUITS

Makes about 20

Preheat oven to 450°. Sift together:

**2 cups flour**
**3 teaspoons baking powder**

Combine with:

**½ cup ground cooked Virginia
or Country ham**

Cut in with knife till it is like meal:

**3 tablespoons shortening**

Add:

**¾ cup milk**

Roll out ¼ inch thick, on a floured board. Cut out with a biscuit cutter. Place on an ungreased baking sheet. Bake 12 to 15 minutes or until brown.

---

## POPOVERS FONTAINE

Makes 8

If you have never had the thrill of seeing a "runny" batter bloom into a large golden cloud, try this recipe. Popovers are definitely a Sunday morning breakfast treat. Serve with fried ham and scrambled eggs. Butter generously and top with honey or syrup.

Preheat oven to 400°. Lightly grease:

**8 five ounce custard cups or
an old-fashioned popover pan**

In a medium bowl, with a rotary beater, beat until well combined:

**3 eggs**
**1 cup milk**
**3 tablespoons salad oil or
melted butter**

Sift into egg mixture:

**1 cup flour**
**½ teaspoon salt**

Beat just until smooth. Pour batter into greased custard cups, filling each half full. Place cups on a baking sheet and bake 45 to 50 minutes, until golden brown. Serve at once.

---

## CRACKLIN' BREAD

Cracklin' bread is made from cracklings, the crisp brown pieces of pork fat remaining after lard has been rendered. It was originally made of salt, corn meal, water and cracklings. However this recipe, like many old recipes, has been refined and now uses buttermilk.

Combine in a bowl:

**3 cups corn meal**
**1 teaspoon salt**

**1 teaspoon soda**
**¼ cup shortening**
**2 cups cracklings**

Stir in enough to make a stiff batter:

**about ¾ cup buttermilk**

Heat an iron skillet containing 1 teaspoon grease until it is very hot. Spread batter in hot skillet and bake at 400° until golden brown, about 20 to 25 minutes.

# GRANDMAMA JONES' ROLLS

Makes 36

*Step One:* Place in a mixing bowl:

**1 cup warm water**
**¼ cup sugar**

Sprinkle over the water and stir until dissolved:

**1 package dry yeast**

*Step Two:* Stir in:

**½ stick softened margarine or 4 tablespoons softened shortening**

*Step Three:* Sift and measure:

**3½ cups flour**

Beat in, with electric mixer, one half of the flour and:

**1 teaspoon salt**
**1 egg**

Gradually add rest of flour; mix well and turn dough out on floured surface. Knead until it is not sticky, adding more flour, if necessary.

*Step Four:* Grease a bowl heavily with:

**margarine or shortening**

Place dough in bowl and whirl around until dough is well coated with margarine. Turn dough over so greased side is up. Cover bowl with wax paper and dish towel and place in a warm place out of drafts. Let rise until double in bulk.

*Step Five:* Punch down and knead dough. Roll into balls or desired shapes and place in heavily greased pan. Pat down balls. Brush with melted butter. Cover with wax paper and towel. Place in warm place to let rolls rise. When double in bulk and ready to bake, place in 400° oven for 15 minutes or until brown. When rolls brown slightly, you can brush again with melted butter and continue browning for a nice tender crust.

# EDNA'S HOT ROLLS

Makes 48

Mrs. W. G. Saunders, Jr., of Meadowbrook Farm, whose home appears on the cover of this book, shared with me her favorite roll recipe.

*Step One:* Preheat oven to 350°. Dissolve and mix well in a large bowl:

**2 yeast cakes or 2 packages active dry yeast**
**1 cup sugar**

Add and set bowl aside:

**4 egg yolks**

**2 cups lukewarm milk**

*Step Two:* In another bowl blend:

**5 cups flour**
**1½ cups shortening**
**1 teaspoon salt**

Fold flour mixture into egg mixture.

*Step Three:* Beat until stiff:

**4 egg whites**

Fold into above mixture well, cover and let rise for at least 1 to 1½ hours. Spoon on floured pastry sheet. Put a little flour on your hands and form into rolls. Place rolls on a greased baking sheet and let rise again until double in bulk. Bake at 350° for approximately 15 minutes or until browned. If you do not want to bake these the same day they are made, freeze them after the dough has been shaped and placed on the baking sheet. Once frozen, store in a plastic bag until ready to use; remove from freezer, place on a baking sheet, let thaw until double, and bake as directed.

## FRENCH BREAD

Makes 2 loaves

As a teen, I used to babysit for Mr. and Mrs. Charles McElroy's two sons. The home was always laden with the aroma of freshly baked French bread. As a new bride, one of my first culinary efforts was to obtain her time-tested recipe to begin my collection.

*Step One:* Combine in a large mixing bowl:

**2 tablespoons shortening**
**1 tablespoon salt**
**1 tablespoon sugar**
**1 cup boiling water**

Stir and add:

**1 cup cold water**

Cool mixture to lukewarm. Sprinkle over mixture and let stand 5 minutes:

**2 packages active dry yeast**

*Step Two:* Beat in gradually 5 cups of:

**6 to 6½ cups sifted all purpose flour, hard wheat preferable**

Turn stiff dough out onto a floured board and knead until the dough is smooth and elastic. Add remaining flour at this time, if necessary, to make dough that does not stick to hands or board. Place dough in a well-greased bowl. Grease the top of the dough with:

**soft shortening**

*Step Three:* Cover with wax paper and a towel and place in a warm place, free from drafts, to rise. Let rise about 1 to 1½ hours or until double in bulk; punch down. Let rise about 30 more minutes. Turn onto a board and knead slightly to press out gas bubbles. Divide dough in two equal parts. Shape each part into a long cylinder shape almost as long as the diagonal of a large baking sheet. Place each loaf on a baking sheet which has been greased and sprinkled with corn meal. With a sharp knife make shallow diagonal slashes across the top of the loaves. Brush with:

**slightly beaten egg white**

*Step Four:* Let rise, uncovered, in a warm place, free from drafts, for about 1 to 1½ hours or until double in bulk. Bake in a 375° oven for 20 minutes. Brush once again with egg white and continue baking for 5 more minutes or until the crust is a rich golden brown color. Remove from oven and remove from baking sheets immediately. Turn off oven, but while it is still hot return loaves to oven rack for 5 to 10 minutes to harden crust. Cool on wire racks or a wooden pastry board in a drafty place.

Use leftovers for French toast with a little Grand Marnier liqueur poured over it; sprinkle with sugar and a bit of jelly for a typical French dessert.

# SOURDOUGH STARTER

Sourdough bread is one of the oldest known breads that families have found wholesome and delicious for centuries. It is made from a starter (a yeast mixture that is self-perpetuating). The starter is the fermenting of flour, water and sugar. Many stories have evolved around sourdough. One describes an Alaskan prospector who always carried his *Sourdough Starter* with him in a tiny pot so he could make bread without having to go a hundred miles to get yeast. Another account was of a western cowpoke cook who always slept with his starter on cold wintery nights so the fermentation action would not stop. He could then depend on hot bread for the morning meal. You will need to make a starter, get one from a friend or purchase it before making the bread.

To make *Sourdough Starter,* scald a crockery, glass or heavy duty plastic bowl or pot. Place in the room temperature bowl:

**2 cups flour**

Add:

**2½ cups lukewarm water**
**2 tablespoons sugar**

Cover with a loose fitting lid. Place in a warm place free from drafts for 3 to 4 days or until fermented. Once you obtain a starter, feed the following mixture to it every 5 to 7 days. Keep in refrigerator in a plastic or glass container. Combine:

**1 cup flour**
**1 cup milk**
**¼ cup sugar**

If you need to use a starter on the same day it is made, you must sprinkle:

**1 package active dry yeast**

Over:

**2 cups flour**

Mix in:

**2½ cups lukewarm water**

This takes only a few hours to ferment and then is ready to use.

# SOURDOUGH BREAD

Makes 2 loaves or 36 rolls

Once you obtain or make a *Sourdough Starter* you will be able to make a wholesome bread your family will enjoy piping hot.

*Step One:* To make bread, combine in a large bowl:

**1 cup** *Sourdough Starter*

**1 package dry yeast**
**½ cup warm water**
**1 tablespoon sugar**

Let cool, then add:

**1 egg**
**2 teaspoons salt**
**5 tablespoons plus 1 teaspoon sugar**

**5 to 6 cups flour**
**1 cup warm water**

*Step Two:* Mix above ingredients together well; cover and let rise 1½ to 2 hours. Punch dough down and put in buttered loaf pans or make rolls. Cover and let rise until doubled in bulk. Bake at 350° for 20 minutes.

---

## LUNDY'S WHOLE WHEAT SOURDOUGH BREAD

---

Makes 2 loaves or 36 rolls

For the nutrition conscious, an unbleached flour contains more vitamins. Try this wholesome bread sliced with ham and spread with spicey mustard. This is the kind of loaf you will want to keep in your kitchen at all times as does my friend Lundy Nicholson. For Christmas gifts, Lundy gives this recipe attached to a crockery pot containing 1 cup of *Sourdough Starter*. Her friends can then feed their own starter and bake this bread...a clever, original gift. Use our *Sourdough Starter* recipe if you don't have your own. Unbleached all-purpose flour will make this even more nutritious.

*Step One:* Dissolve:

**1 package dry yeast**
**1 tablespoon sugar**
**½ cup warm water**

*Step Two:* Add:

**½ cup melted butter**
**1 cup** *Sourdough Starter*

Let cool a few minutes, then add:

**1 egg**
**½ cup sugar**
**4 cups plus 5 tablespoons**
  **all-purpose flour**
**1 cup whole wheat flour**
**2 teaspoons salt**
**1 cup water**

Mix all together.

*Step Three:* Cover and place bowl in warm place, free from drafts. Let rise about 1½ to 2 hours. Punch down and put in a buttered loaf pan, or shape into rolls and place in roll pan. Cover. Let rise again until double in bulk, about 1½ to 2 hours. Bake at 350° for 20 minutes.

# GREAT AUNTIE'S FOOLPROOF LOAF BREAD

Makes 2 loaves

Brooks Godwin, a former home economics student of mine, shared with me this foolproof recipe that was her Great Aunt's. It is absolutely delicious and it also freezes well.

Place in a large bowl:

**1½ cups warm water**

Add:

**¼ cup sugar or molasses**
**1 cup corn meal or wheat germ or rolled oats**

Sprinkle over above mixture:

**1 package active dry yeast**

Let stand 10 minutes. In a separate bowl combine:

**1 to 2 teaspoons salt**
**2 egg yolks**
**5 tablespoons plus 1 teaspoon corn oil**
**1 cup dry milk**

Combine mixtures. Add and gradually stir in:

**4 cups flour**

Cover. Set in warm place 30 minutes. Knead lightly. Cover and let double in bulk. Turn out and shape into two loaves. Place in greased pans size 5 by 3 by 6 or 2 by 4 by 8 inches and let rise until double in bulk. Put in a cold oven; put a shallow pan of water on the bottom rack. Turn oven to 350° and bake 40 to 50 minutes. Turn out and cool.

# JULE KAGA
## (CHRISTMAS SCANDINAVIAN BREAD)

Makes 2 loaves

Peggy Christensen Hopewell gave me her traditional Scandinavian Christmas fruit bread recipe that has been in her family for generations. The Danes are great coffee drinkers, and this is served not only for breakfast, but as a snack with afternoon coffee. It will also grace a more formal coffee table along with Danish ham sandwiches or our traditional ham biscuits. Try this toasted and buttered on the second day.

*Step One:* Dissolve:

**1 cake yeast or 1 package active dry yeast**
**½ cup warm water**

*Step Two:* In another large bowl place:

**½ cup sugar**

Pour over:

**1½ cups scalded milk**

*Step Three:* Melt, then set aside to cool:

**¾ stick butter (not margarine)**

*Step Four:* When milk is lukewarm, add the yeast mixture. Sift onto waxed paper:

**4½ to 5 cups flour**

Add to milk mixture one half of the flour and:

**1 teaspoon salt**

Add the cooled butter and:

**2 eggs**

Beat 10 minutes with an electric beater.

*Step Five:* Add the rest of the flour and:

**¼ cup chopped citrin and
¼ cup chopped candied cherries
or ½ cup chopped mixed
candied fruit
¾ cup raisins
12 or less cardamom seeds**

Knead well. Place in a greased bowl. Cover and set in a warm place to rise until double in bulk. Punch down, cover and let rise again until double. Shape into loaves and place into 2 greased loaf pans or 2 greased round layer cake pans. Cover pans. Let rise until double in bulk. Bake at 350° for 35 to 40 minutes. Remove from pan and brush with:

**melted butter**

Sprinkle with:

**cinnamon
sugar**

## QUICK WHOLE WHEAT BREAD

Makes 1 loaf

This is nutritious as well as easy.

Sift into a bowl:

**¼ cup all purpose flour
1 teaspoon baking powder
1 teaspoon baking soda
1 teaspoon salt**

Add:

**2 cups whole wheat flour**

**½ cup cracked rye
1½ cups sour milk
½ cup molasses
¼ cup melted shortening**

Stir well. Spoon into a buttered 9 by 5 inch loaf pan. Allow to stand for 20 minutes. Bake at 375° for about 50 minutes.

To make sweet milk sour, stir in lemon juice or vinegar, 1 tablespoon to a cup, and let stand for a few minutes.

# APPETIZERS, SOUPS, AND SALADS

Appetizers are a popular twentieth century way of serving the first course of a meal, entertaining guests on the lawn, or enhancing the more festive cocktail party. Our ancestors invited guests for dinner which generally did not include appetizers. Many other countries, however, have had counterparts to our appetizers for centuries: Russia's *zakuski*, Italy's *antipasto*, Denmark's *koldu bord*, and France's *hors d'oeuvres*, but the most well known is Sweden's *smorgasbord*. The latter may be a meal in itself today, but its origin as the eighteenth century "aquavit buffet" was the introduction to a festive Swedish meal. It was set on a separate table in the corner of the dining room or adjoining room and was enjoyed by the guests while standing before being seated for dinner. The *smorgasbord* table was usually laden with salty foods so as to whet the appetite.

Ham, being salty, lends itself to making many varieties of tasty appetizers. The more popular appetizer is the ham biscuit that is often served to visiting dignitaries in Williamsburg as well as in homes all over the American South. Those leftover bits and pieces of ham, ground or minced, can find their way into such delectables as *Ham-Stuffed Mushrooms, Ham Log, Mini-Ham Pizzas,* or endless other dishes to stimulate and enhance the appetites of your guests.

# APPETIZERS

## QUICK APPETIZER HAM WRAPS

For a quick appetizer use ham and an assortment of foods that you may have on hand. Wrap thin strips of ham one inch wide around any of the following, or improvise your own fillings, and secure with colored toothpicks:

> **cheese cubes**
> **melon balls**
> **cream cheese-stuffed dates**
> **watermelon pickle**
> **pineapple chunks**
> **sweet cucumber pickles**
> **avocado cubes**

> **olives**
> **marinated artichoke hearts**
> **cocktail cherry tomatoes**
> **cooked shrimp**

Stick these in a pineapple or a red head of cabbage for a colorful arrangement. At Christmas, cover a styrofoam tree with aluminum foil, then stick the ham wraps into it. Place sprigs of parsley around the wraps for an authentic-looking tree. Guests may help themselves.

## GRACE'S MEAT BALLS

Makes about 36

Mix and blend well:

> **½ cup ground cooked ham**
> **1 tablespoon creamy peanut butter**

Add and mix well with the ham:

> **1 pound ground chuck**

Cut into small pieces:

> **½ pound bleu cheese**

Mold and shape the ground meat mixture around the bleu cheese, forming small balls. Place balls in a glass, china, or crockery bowl, and pour over them:

> **about ¼ cup dry red wine**

Let stand in refrigerator for 3 hours. Remove balls from dish, brown in a non-stick pan. Remove to chafing dish or serving platter. Serve on toothpicks.

# SUFFOLK PEANUT-HAM BALLS

Makes 24

Combine in a small bowl:

**1 cup finely ground cooked
Virginia or Country ham
5 to 6 tablespoons mayonnaise
1 tablespoon Dijon mustard**

Mix thoroughly and shape into balls. Stuff one of each in the center of each ball:

**24 peanuts**

Roll each ball in:

**¼ cup fine bread crumbs**

Fry quickly in deep hot fat until golden. Drain on paper towels. Serve warm.

# VIRGINIA HAM-CHICKEN TEMPTERS

Makes 40

Nice for a cocktail buffet!

Preheat oven to 325°. Bone and flatten:

**8 chicken breast halves**

Layer on each half breast one half slice of:

**4 slices Virginia or Country ham**

Roll up tightly and secure with toothpick. Place in casserole dish. Top with a sauce made by combining:

**1 ten ounce can cream of
mushroom soup
4 to 6 ounces dry sherry**

Bake for about 1 hour. Allow to cool. Slice rolls into bite-size pieces and serve on toothpicks. They can be placed in a chafing dish with a little sauce, after you have sliced them.

# HAM AND ASPARAGUS ROLLS

Makes 32

Preheat oven to 400°. Remove crust and roll flat:

**16 slices bread**

Brush both sides lightly with:

**¼ cup melted butter**

Drain:

**2 one pound cans asparagus tips**

Have ready enough ham to make:

**16 sandwich size squares sliced cooked ham**

Place on each slice of buttered bread 1 asparagus tip and 1 slice of ham. Roll up and secure with toothpicks and cut each roll in half. Place on a baking sheet and bake 8 to 10 minutes until lightly browned. Serve at once. These rolls can be left whole and served for lunch, topped with a cheese or mushroom sauce.

# EASY HAM ROLLS

Makes 16

Open:

**1 eight ounce can refrigerator crescent rolls**

Divide rolls according to package directions. Cut each pastry triangle in half. Sprinkle wide end of each triangle with one tablespoon of:

**1 cup ground cooked ham**

Roll, starting at wide end. Bake, according to package directions, on ungreased baking sheet.

# HAM CRESCENT ROLL-UPS

Makes 24

Preheat oven to 375°. Open:

**1 eight ounce package crescent rolls**

Press edges together to form a square from 2 of the triangular-shaped rolls. Spread each square with:

**hot mustard**

Sprinkle about 3 tablespoons of each of the following on each square:

**1½ cups chopped cooked ham**
**1½ cups grated sharp Cheddar cheese**

Roll up like a jelly roll and cut into one-fourth inch slices. Place on an ungreased cookie sheet. Bake 10 to 12 minutes. Serve immediately.

# HAM PUFFS

Makes 16

Combine:

**3 tablespoons mayonnaise**
**½ cup ground ham**
**2 hard-cooked eggs, chopped**
**1 tablespoon prepared mustard**

Open:

**1 eight ounce package refrigerator crescent rolls**

Cut triangle rolls in half. Spoon a little ham filling into each triangle and seal closed, making a turnover. Drop puffs into hot oil for 1 minute or until lightly browned. Drain and serve with hot mustard.

# VIRGINIA HAM WAFERS

Makes about 36

Good with salads, soups and drinks.

Preheat oven to 350°. Sift together:

**2 cups flour**
**2 teaspoons baking powder**
**⅛ teaspoon cayenne pepper**

Cut in with a knife, then mix well:

**1 cup margarine**

**1 cup grated sharp cheese**
**½ cup chopped cooked Virginia or Country ham**

Pinch off small pieces and place on ungreased cookie sheet and pat flat. Bake for 15 minutes. To make ham straws, roll dough very thin, cut in strips about ¼ inch wide and 4 inches long.

# DIXIE PINWHEELS

Makes 24

Preheat Oven to 425°. Combine:

**2 cups packaged biscuit mix**
**scant ¾ cup milk**

Mix lightly with a fork and turn onto floured surface. Roll dough ¼ inch thick to form a rectangle, 8 by 14 inches.

Mix together:

**1 cup ground cooked ham**
**2 tablespoons mayonnaise**
**1 teaspoon prepared mustard**

Spread this mixture over dough and roll up like a jellyroll. Cut into ¼ inch pieces. Place on a slightly greased baking sheet and bake for 15 to 20 minutes.

## HAM AND CHEESE SPIRALS

Makes 30

Preheat oven to 400°. Sift together:

**¾ cup flour**
**½ teaspoon salt**

Cut in with a knife:

**6 tablespoons grated cheese**
**2 tablespoons margarine**

Add and mix well:

**3 to 4 tablespoons milk**

Roll pastry out in a rectangle and spread with:

**about 6 ounces ground cooked ham**

Roll up like a jelly roll. Chill for 2 hours; slice thin. Bake on a cookie sheet for 10 minutes.

## HAM AND CHEESE MARBLES

Makes 40

These make a nice tray for a tea or reception. Serve piping hot.

Preheat oven to 350°. In mixing bowl, combine:

**½ cup butter**
**1½ cups shredded Cheddar cheese**
**¼ cup finely chopped baked ham**

**¼ teaspoon Worcestershire sauce**
**dash cayenne**

Blend in:

**1 cup sifted all-purpose flour**

Shape dough into a smooth ball. Roll dough into balls the size of large marbles. Place on an ungreased baking sheet. Bake for 15 to 18 minutes.

## CHEESE PUFFS SURPRISE

Makes 24

Preheat oven to 400°. Cut:

**24 ham cubes**

Blend:

**¼ pound grated sharp cheese**
**¼ pound butter**

Add and blend into a soft dough:

**½ cup flour**

**½ teaspoon paprika**

Pinch off about ½ teaspoon dough and shape around each ham cube, covering it completely. Refrigerate at least 4 to 5 hours. Overnight is better, and they will keep in the refrigerator for one week before baking. Bake on an ungreased cookie sheet for 10 to 15 minutes.

# CINDY'S NIBBLERS

Makes 32

Mix:

**1 eight ounce package cream
cheese**
**2 tablespoons mayonnaise**
**2 tablespoons chopped olives**
**1 teaspoon prepared mustard**

Spread on:

**8 slices cooked ham**

Roll up each slice, secure with tooth-picks, and refrigerate for several hours until well chilled. Slice and serve on crackers. Instead of mixing olives and mustard with the cream cheese, omit and place two small whole sweet gherkin pickles on each cream cheese spread slice of ham. Continue as above. Another variation is to mix ¼ cup drained pineapple with the cream cheese in lieu of olives and mustard.

# HAM AND OLIVE TOPPERS

Makes 20 to 25

Mix together:

**2 tablespoons mayonnaise**
**2 tablespoons chopped olives**
**1 three ounce package cream
cheese**
**1 teaspoon horseradish, drained**
**½ teaspoon mustard**

**¼ teaspoon basil or parsley**

Spread this on:

**4 thin slices ham**

Roll up jelly-roll fashion and secure with toothpicks. Chill for several hours, slice into ¼ inch slices and place on crackers.

# HAM-SWISS WHEELS

Makes about 60

Mix:

**½ cup commercial onion dip**
**2 tablespoons chopped ripe olives**
**1 three ounce package cream
cheese, softened**

Spread mixture evenly on:

**12 slices cooked ham**

Top with:

**12 slices Swiss cheese**

Spread with more dip, roll each ham slice, fasten with a toothpick, and wrap in waxed paper. Chill at least 2 hours; then cut each roll into ½ inch slices. Serve on favorite cracker.

# HAM CAPERS

Makes about 30

Mix well:

**1 eight ounce package cream
cheese
2 teaspoons capers
dash onion salt
dash garlic salt**

**2 tablespoons half and half**

Spread this mixture over:

**7 or 8 ham slices**

Roll up each slice like a jelly roll. Chill until firm, slice and serve on favorite crackers.

# HAM CHUTNEY TWIRLS

Makes about 30

Soften until spreading consistency:

**1 three ounce package cream
cheese
1 tablespoon mayonnaise**

Spread mixture among:

**6 slices cooked ham**

Spread on top:

**½ to ¾ cup chutney**

Roll up each slice jelly-roll fashion and secure with a toothpick. Chill until firm and slice half an inch thick. Serve with your favorite crackers.

# HAM AND PEPPER SLICES

Makes about 32

Blend together:

**1 eight ounce package cream
cheese
½ cup chopped olives
2 tablespoons mayonnaise
½ cup chopped pecans
1 cup cooked ground ham
2 tablespoons chopped pimiento**

Cut stem end off, carefully remove

seeds and ribs from:

**8 small green peppers (about 2
inches wide)**

Stuff ham mixture into the dry green peppers. Chill until firm. Slice peppers crosswise and serve on your favorite cracker. For variety substitute ¼ cup drained crushed pineapple in place of olives and ¼ cup drained chopped maraschino cherries in place of pimiento.

# HAM-STUFFED CHERRY TOMATOES

Makes 40

Cut a very thin slice off the top of each of:

**40 cherry tomatoes**

Scoop out pulp, invert and drain on paper towel. Combine with tomato pulp:

**1 cup ground ham**

**4 ounces softened cream cheese**
**2 tablespoons grated onion**
**2 tablespoons minced celery**

Stuff mixture into tomatoes with a small spoon. These make a colorful and delicious appetizer. Make them ahead of time and chill before serving. Stuff cherry tomatoes with *Virginia Ham Salad* for another treat.

# HAM-STUFFED MUSHROOMS

Makes 12 servings

A friend, Ms. Beth Polson, Los Angeles television writer and newspaper columnist, gave us this recipe. It is one of our favorite hors d'oeuvres.

Preheat oven to 325°. Remove and chop stems and wipe with a dry cloth:

**12 large mushrooms or**
**24 bite-size mushrooms**

Melt:

**2 tablespoons butter**

Sauté in butter until tender:

chopped mushroom stems
**¼ cup chopped onion**

Combine with mushroom mixture:

**1 cup ground or finely minced Country ham**
**1 cup dry bread crumbs**
**1 slightly beaten egg**

Stuff caps, add a sliver of pimiento for color. Bake 15 minutes, or broil until done, if you prefer. These also make a pretty accompaniment to a main course. For a variation of stuffing, see *Suffolk Peanut and Ham Spread.*

# NANCY LAINE'S APPETIZER HAM BALL

This can be made several days ahead and refrigerated.

Grind:

**1 cup cooked ham**

Add and blend:

**3 tablespoons chopped stuffed green olives**

**1 tablespoon prepared mustard**
**Tabasco to taste**
**1 three ounce package softened cream cheese**
**2 teaspoons milk**

Form into a ball and chill at least 15 minutes before serving. Trim with parsley or roll ball in chopped parsley.

# HAM FRUIT BALL

Very colorful holiday appetizer that can be made several days ahead. It freezes very well.

Blend together:

**1 eight ounce package cream cheese**
**½ cup well drained mandarin oranges**
**½ cup well drained crushed pineapple**
**½ cup chopped maraschino cherries**

Add:

**1 cup ground ham**

Combine then sprinkle on a piece of waxed paper:

**1 cup pecan meal and ½ cup chopped pecans or 1½ cups pecan-flavored peanuts**

Form mixture into a ball and roll in nuts. Garnish top of ball with whole cherries. Chill and serve with crackers.

# PINEAPPLE - HAM - CHEESE BALL

This is a spicy appetizer. A dash of ground ginger or horseradish will make a spicier ball. Serve with favorite crackers.

Stir until soft and creamy or use *cream* setting on mixer:

**1 eight ounce package cream cheese**

Drain, reserving juice:

**1 eight ounce can crushed pineapple**

Add gradually to cheese the pineapple and enough pineapple juice to make mixture spreading consistency, then add:

**1 cup ground ham**

Chill until cold enough to form into a ball. Roll in:

**1 cup chopped pecans**

Refrigerate until ready to use.

## HAM LOG

This has a unique flavor that will inspire your guests to ask for the recipe. It can be made several days before using and kept in the refrigerator. It freezes well.

Soften:

**1 eight ounce package cream cheese**

Blend in with a fork:

**1 tablespoon mayonnaise**

**½ cup chopped chutney**
**1 cup ground cooked ham**

Shape into log form. Sprinkle on waxed paper:

**1 cup chopped pecans or pecan-flavored peanuts**

Roll log in this nut mixture until well covered. Wrap in foil and chill until firm. Garnish with cherries and serve with crackers.

## FROZEN LOG

This is delicious for hors d'oeuvres or great for lunch when spread on a split English muffin, then broiled.

Put through a food chopper:

**½ pound yellow sharp cheese**
**¼ to ½ cup cooked ham**
**½ teaspoon Worcestershire sauce**

**2 small onions**
**1 teaspoon dry mustard**
**2 teaspoons mayonnaise**

Mix and shape into a log that is two inches in diameter. Freeze until ready to serve, slice and put on melba rounds or your favorite cracker. Put under broiler until brown.

# VIRGINIA HAM PATE

Makes 1½ cups

Combine in a small bowl:

    **1 cup ground cooked ham**
    **2 hard-cooked eggs,**
    **very finely chopped**
    **1 three ounce package softened**
    **cream cheese**
    **1 teaspoon Dijon mustard**

    **2 or 3 truffles or mushrooms,**
    **finely chopped**
    **1 tablespoon finely minced onion**

Place in blender and give a whirl. Serve on cheese wafers or warm cocktail biscuits (*Grandma Preece's Buttermilk Biscuits*).

# SUFFOLK PEANUT AND HAM SPREAD

Preheat oven to 350°. Put in blender and blend until smooth:

    **½ cup sour cream**
    **1 cup finely minced ham**
    **½ cup unsalted peanuts (if ham**
    **is mild, use salted nuts)**
    **2 tablespoons finely minced**
    **onion**

Stuff fresh mushroom caps with the spread and bake 15 minutes. You can use this as a spread for party sandwiches or on crackers. It also makes a delicious dip for vegetables; just add more sour cream to obtain a dip consistency and add more onion to suit taste.

# HAM GLAZED CREAM CHEESE

Place on a small serving tray:

    **1 eight ounce package**
    **cream cheese**

Press lightly into top of cheese:

    **½ cup ground ham**

Spread over the ham:

    **¼ cup hot pepper jelly**

Arrange rice crackers around the glazed cheese and serve. These interesting flavors combine well.

# HAM DREAM CANAPES

Makes 40

Cut out sliced bread with biscuit cutter to prepare about:

**40 biscuit-size rounds of bread**

Melt over low heat:

**2 tablespoons butter**

Stir in:

**2 tablespoons flour**

Gradually add and stir in:

**1 cup milk**

As this begins to thicken, stir in:

**½ cup grated Cheddar cheese**
**½ cup ground or finely chopped cooked ham**
**dash of Worcestershire sauce**

Spread on bread rounds and refrigerate until serving time. Place under broiler and heat thoroughly before serving.

# HAM DIP

Makes 2½ cups

Blend together:

**16 ounces sour cream**
**3 tablespoons mayonnaise**
**1½ teaspoons brown sugar**
**¼ cup chili sauce**
**1 tablespoon mustard**
**1½ teaspoons chili powder**
**1 cup ground ham**

Refrigerate. Serve with potato chips, crackers or fresh raw vegetables. For an attractive serving arrangement, cut out the interior of a red cabbage, leaving about 1 inch thick sides, to form a bowl. Fill the cavity with dip. Arrange on a platter, surrounded with vegetables for dipping.

# HOT COUNTRY HAM DIP

Preheat oven to 350°. Combine in a small bowl and place in a baking dish:

**2 eight ounce packages cream cheese, softened**

**1 cup sour cream**

**½ to 1 cup chopped, cooked Country ham**

**¼ cup finely minced onion**

**½ teaspoon garlic powder**

Sauté and sprinkle over baking dish:

**1 tablespoon butter**

**1 cup chopped pecans**

**½ teaspoon Worcestershire sauce**

Refrigerate until serving time. Bake for 20 minutes. Serve hot with crackers or raw crisp vegetables. For a group of six, halve the recipe.

# HAM CURRY DIP

Makes about 1½ cups

Blend together:

**½ cup ground or finely minced ham**

**½ cup sour cream**

**½ cup mayonnaise**

**dash Tabasco**

**2 teaspoons curry powder**

**1 teaspoon lemon juice**

**4 tablespoons grated onion**

**½ teaspoon Worcestershire sauce**

**3 tablespoons ketchup**

Chill and serve with raw vegetables.

# INDIVIDUAL HAM QUICHES

Makes 36

This is a gourmet treat your special guests will appreciate.

Preheat oven to 425°. In a small bowl cream:

**1 three ounce package cream cheese, softened**

**1 stick butter, softened**

Work into the mixture:

**1 cup unsifted flour**

Wrap dough in wax paper and refrigerate for 30 minutes. Pinch bits of dough off, roll into balls, about 1 inch in diameter. Press each ball into miniature muffin or tart tins, working the dough with the thumbs and turning the tin clockwise at the same time. The pastry should be ⅛ inch thick. Work all of dough into pastry shells.

Chop finely and combine:

**1 cup cooked ham**

**¼ cup grated Swiss or Gruyere cheese**

Put 1 teaspoon of minced ham mixture in each pastry shell. Combine:

**2 slightly beaten eggs**
**1 cup heavy cream**
**dash pepper**

Fill each shell with the liquid mixture; do not over fill. Sprinkle with:

**grated Parmesan cheese**

Bake for 5 minutes. Reduce temperature to 350° and bake 15 minutes longer. The quiches should be set and lightly browned. Serve immediately.

## MINI HAM PIZZAS

These can be made in just a few minutes and are so delicious.

Brush:

**bottled chili sauce**

On:

**Ritz crackers**

Spread each cracker with:

**1 teaspoon ground ham**

Top with:

**cracker size cheese squares**

Sprinkle with:

**ground oregano**

Put under the broiler until cheese melts.

## HAM AND PINEAPPLE KABOBS

8 servings

Peel and cut into bite-size cubes:

**1 pineapple**

Or drain thoroughly:

**1 thirteen ounce can pineapple cubes**

Soak overnight in:

**¼ cup port wine**

Cut in cubes:

**1 pound cooked ham**

Skewer cubes of ham and pineapple on toothpicks and stick in a grapefruit to serve, or serve on a bed of freshly grated or toasted coconut for a first course.

# HAM KABOBS

4 servings

Kabob cookery originated in the middle Eastern countries centuries ago. Today it is a popular way of preparing meat chunks with fruit or vegetables threaded on skewers, then charcoaled or broiled. These may also be threaded on skewers and served over rice with *Sweet and Sour Sauce*.

Drain, reserving ¼ cup juice:

> **1 thirteen ounce can pineapple chunks**

Melt in pan:

> **½ cup butter**

Stir in along with reserved pineapple juice:

> **2 tablespoons lemon juice**
> **3 tablespoons brown sugar**

> **⅛ teaspoon ground cloves**
> **⅛ teaspoon dry mustard**

Cook and stir until sauce is heated through. Thread onto skewers along with drained pineapple chunks:

> **1 large orange, sectioned or**
> **1 can mandarin oranges, drained**
> **1 pound cubed cooked ham**
> **1 six ounce jar maraschino cherries**

Broil for 5 minutes, turning and basting with sauce. Serve on toothpicks as appetizers, sticking the picks in a pineapple for guests to help themselves. Guests enjoy grilling and basting their own over a miniature hibachi.

# HAM AND CHEESE FONDUE

Makes 2¾ cups

This is easy to prepare, and is always popular with guests. Any leftovers can be served over toast for breakfast.

Melt in saucepan and cook for two minutes:

> **2½ tablespoons butter**
> **3 tablespoons instant flour**

Remove from heat and beat in with a wire whisk:

> **2 cups boiling milk**
> **⅛ teaspoon white pepper**
> **pinch cayenne pepper**

Boil, stirring for one minute. Remove sauce from heat, beat in with wire whisk:

> **1 egg yolk**

Add:

> **½ cup coarsely grated Swiss cheese**
> **½ cup minced cooked ham**
> **dash salt (omit if Country ham is used)**

Serve at once with cubed French bread. If not used immediately, dot top of sauce with butter to prevent a skim from forming. This can also be used as a delicious filling for turnovers and crepes by reducing milk to 1½ cups.

# SOUPS

Some folks consider the hambone to be the whole point of the ham. It is the key to getting that delicious flavor into a dish that would otherwise make a drab meal. The hambone is the inspiration for the best of homemade soups that are so great on a cold winter's day. A great way to finish a ham!

## HAM AND PEA SOUP

Doris Miller, wife of the Attorney General of Virginia, Andrew Miller, says her family declares that her soup is the "best part of a ham."

Put in a soup pot and simmer for several hours until good and thick, stirring occasionally:

**1 hambone with some meat on it**

**1 package split green peas (not preflavored)**
**1 large onion, cut in chunks**
**about 1 dozen peppercorns**
**about a quart water**

Put through a sieve, remove bones and pick out nice bits of ham to put back in soup. This will keep several days in the refrigerator; just heat and serve.

## QUICK VEGETABLE HAMBONE SOUP

Makes 8 to 10 servings

Place in soup pot:

**1 quart water**
**1 hambone**

Bring to a boil and simmer for 30 minutes. Add:

**1 pound can lima beans**
**1 pound can mixed vegetables**

**1 cup uncooked macaroni shells**
**1 pound can corn**

Cook until macaroni is almost done, then add:

**2 eight ounce cans tomato sauce**
**¼ cup sugar**
**salt and pepper to taste**

Cook until macaroni is done; serve.

# ROSA'S HAMBONE SOUP

Makes 8 to 10 servings

Place in pot:

**1 cooked Country hambone**
**2 cups water**

Bring to a boil, then simmer about 30 minutes. Remove hambone, cool until you can handle it, then remove all meat.

Add to pot along with meat removed from ham bone, the following vegetables—the more the merrier:

**1 cup chopped celery**
**2 cups chopped white potatoes**
**1 cup chopped carrots**

**1 cup shelled butterbeans or**
**  1 pound can butterbeans**
**2 medium onions, chopped**
**5 fresh tomatoes, chopped**
**1 cup water**

If using canned tomatoes (1 lb. can) omit extra water. Simmer for 20 minutes.

Add:

**corn cut from 5 ears or**
**  1 pound can corn**

Season with:

**black pepper to taste**
**1 tablespoon sugar**

Simmer 15 more minutes and serve.

# BLACK BEAN SOUP

6 to 8 servings

This makes a nice soup course for a formal dinner.

Soak overnight in cold water to cover:

**2 cups dried black beans**

Drain and place in soup pot with:

**hambone with meat or ham hock**
**2 quarts water**
**2 medium onions, chopped**
**3 carrots, diced**
**4 stalks celery with leaves, diced**
**5 sprigs parsley**
**3 whole cloves**
**1 clove garlic**
**2 bay leaves**
**1 tablespoon Worcestershire sauce**

**1 teaspoon dry mustard**
**pinch allspice**
**pinch thyme**

Bring to boil, reduce heat, simmer for 2½ to 3 hours or until beans are very tender. Remove ham and bone; cut meat into small pieces. Work soup through a sieve or blend in an electric blender. Add diced ham and:

**¼ cup sherry or dry Madeira**
**salt and pepper to taste**

If soup is too thick, add a little water; it should be the consistency of heavy cream. Reheat before serving and garnish with:

**2 hard cooked eggs, sliced**
**thin slices lemon**

# BEAN SOUP

8 to 10 servings

Soak overnight:

**1 pound navy beans**

Place in soup pot:

**1 quart water**
**1 cooked hambone**

Cook for about an hour. Add the beans and cook approximately 2 hours. Add:

**1 thirty-two ounce can tomatoes**
**3 carrots, sliced**
**2 to 3 medium onions, chopped**

Cook for about 30 minutes and serve.

# NAVY BEAN SOUP

8 to 10 servings

A Country hambone can be stored wrapped in foil in the refrigerator up to three months and on any cold day can be the inspiration for this soup.

Soak overnight in cold water:

**1 pound navy beans**

Place in soup pot with drained navy beans:

**1 baked country hambone or
ham hock**
**3 quarts water**

Bring to a boil, then reduce heat and simmer 4 to 5 hours. If you prefer a spicier soup after 2 hours of cooking add:

**2 tablespoons diced celery
(optional)**
**2 tablespoons diced onion
(optional)**
**1 tablespoon chopped parsley
(optional)**
**½ small red pepper (optional)**

Continue cooking. Beans will be very, very tender. Add:

**salt and pepper to taste**

# SPANISH GARBANZO BEAN SOUP

4 servings

Soak overnight in sufficient water to cover beans:

>   **1 pound garbanzo beans**
>   **1 tablespoon salt—omit if
>   Country hambone is used**

When ready to cook, drain the salted water from the beans and put the beans in a soup pot with:

>   **1 hambone**
>   **1 beefbone**
>   **2 quarts water**

Bring to a boil, reduce heat and simmer for 45 minutes. Meanwhile fry:

>   **4 slices white bacon**
>   **dash paprika**
>   **1 medium onion, finely chopped**

Add to soup pot along with:

>   **1 pound quartered peeled
>   potatoes**
>   **pinch saffron**

Simmer until potatoes are tender, about 30 minutes. Add:

>   **1 thinly cut Spanish sausage
>   (Chorizos)**

>   **salt to taste**

# HAM AND POTATO SOUP

8 servings

Place in a soup pot:

>   **6 medium potatoes, diced**
>   **1 medium onion, chopped**
>   **1 cup minced cooked ham or
>   ham bits**
>   **1 quart water**

Bring to a boil, reduce heat to low and cook about 20 minutes, until vegetables are tender.

Pour in:

>   **1 ten ounce can cream of
>   celery soup**
>   **1 cup milk**
>   **dash pepper**

Simmer until well blended; serve.

# DIXIE SUMMER SOUP

6 to 8 servings

In a soup pot place:

>   **1 quart cold water**

>   **1 hambone with some meat
>   left on**

Bring to a boil and add:

1 quart tomatoes
1 cup butterbeans
3 medium potatoes, diced
½ cup green beans, broken up
1 cup corn
2 large onions, diced
4 stalks celery, diced

1 tablespoon sugar
   salt and pepper to taste

Simmer 3 hours. Just before serving, mix and add this thickener:

1 egg
1 tablespoon milk
1 teaspoon flour

## VIRGINIA HAM SOUP

8 servings

Judy Pruden of the Pruden ham family, who has had vast experience in cooking with Virginia ham, shared with us her favorite soup recipe.

Dice:

1 pound sliced uncooked Country or Virginia ham

Put into a pot containing:

3 quarts boiling water

Reduce heat and simmer for 1½ hours. Add:

6 white potatoes, diced
1 pound package diced carrots

Cook for 30 minutes. Add:

1 green pepper, diced
1 cup diced celery
2 onions, chopped
1 pound can tomatoes
   salt to taste

Cook for 20 minutes and serve.

## HAM CHOWDER

4 servings

Cook in heavy saucepan until golden brown:

¼ cup chopped onion
1 tablespoon margarine

Add to the pan:

1½ cups hot water
1 cup diced raw potato
⅛ teaspoon pepper
   dash paprika
   dash thyme
1 teaspoon Worcestershire sauce

½ cup chopped cooked smoked or Country ham

Cook 15 minutes on medium heat and add:

2 cups milk

Blend together, then combine with above mixture:

1 tablespoon flour
2 tablespoons water

Simmer until thickened and well blended. Season to taste and serve.

# HAM-FLAVORED BRUNSWICK STEW

8 to 10 servings

Virginians claim that *Brunswick Stew* originated in Brunswick County, Virginia. It was a very popular dish often served at public gatherings. Today, the stew is still being served at public functions such as the homecoming luncheon held on the lawn at the College of William and Mary. It is served in authentic manner from a large black kettle. It has been said that squirrel was the first meat used in making the stew, and now of course chicken is substituted, but it is the old hambone that permeates and gives that rich flavor!

In a large pan put:

**3 pounds chicken, cut up**
**3 quarts water**
**1 large onion, sliced**
**½ pound cooked ham, cut in small pieces, or 1 hambone from a baked Country ham**

Simmer 2 hours. Add:

**3 pints tomatoes**
**1 pint butterbeans**
**4 large potatoes, diced**
**1 pint corn**
**salt to taste**
**¼ teaspoon pepper**
**1 tablespoon chopped parsley**
**2 tablespoons Worcestershire sauce**
**2 teaspoons sugar (optional)**
**1 tablespoon poultry seasoning**

Cover and simmer 2 more hours. Serve with *Sally Lunn* bread. Use canned or frozen vegetables if fresh ones are unavailable. This stew benefits from long slow cooking, and the delectable flavor improves if kept overnight. It is the consistency of mush.

# SALADS

Ham additions can enliven any salad from a fresh vegetable to a congealed one such as *Ham Salad Ring* or *Ham Aspic.* Often it will be the one ingredient that gives your dish that extra zip and encourages your guests to ask for seconds.

## VIRGINIA HAM SALAD

12 servings

This is an old favorite used in the Harrell family for several generations:

Grind:

**2 cups cooked ham**

Mix with the ham:

**1 cup diced celery**

**1 cup diced** *Homemade*

*Cucumber Pickle or* **pickle relish**

**4 hard cooked eggs, chopped fine mayonnaise to moisten**

**1 teaspoon mustard**

Chill and serve on lettuce or in a tomato, avocado, or peach half; or spread on toasted bread for a delicious sandwich.

## STUFFED HAM-TOMATOES

Scoop pulp out of tomatoes and stuff shells with *Virginia Ham Salad.* Serve on lettuce for a tasty lunch.

## QUICK HAM-CHICKEN SALAD

8 servings

Grind or chop in blender:

**1 cup cooked ham**

Cut or grind:

**1 cup cooked chicken**

Mix meats with:

**½ cup chopped celery**

**½ cup** *Homemade Cucumber Pickle or* **pickle relish horseradish to taste**

Add enough to make salad hold together:

**about ½ cup mayonnaise**

Use in sandwiches or on crackers for appetizers.

# HAM WALDORF

6 servings

Peel and chop:

**4 apples**

Combine in a bowl with apples:

**1 cup cubed ham**
**1 cup diced celery**

**1 cup green or Tokay grapes,**
**seeded and halved, or**
**1 cup raisins or both**
**½ cup chopped pecans**

Mix well with enough to moisten:

**about ¾ cup mayonnaise**

Chill well and serve on lettuce leaves.

# HAM-MACARONI SALAD BOWL

10 servings

Bring to a boil:

**3 quarts water**

Add:

**1 teaspoon salt**
**1 eight ounce package macaroni**

Cook until tender, rinse in cold water and drain.

Blend into cooled macaroni:

**1 to 1½ cups diced cooked ham**

**¼ pound Cheddar cheese, diced**
**¼ to ½ cup chopped green pepper**
**¾ cup chopped celery**
**¼ cup chopped onions**
**4 to 6 tablespoons French dressing**
**or mayonnaise**
**½ teaspoon Worcestershire sauce**
**1 chopped tomato**
**salt and pepper to taste**

Garnish with:

**¼ teaspoon paprika**

Chill and serve.

# HAM SALAD RING

8 servings

This ham mold is excellent to serve for a luncheon.

Soften:

**1 envelope unflavored gelatin**
**½ cup chicken broth**

Heat to boiling:

**1 cup chicken broth**

Add gelatin, stirring until dissolved. Remove from heat. Stir in:

**1 tablespoon prepared mustard**
**1 teaspoon Worcestershire sauce**

Cool, then chill until mixture begins to thicken. Add:

**2 tablespoons finely chopped onion**
**5 tablespoons chopped dill or sweet pickle**
**4 tablespoons chopped stuffed green olives**
**1 cup finely chopped cooked Country or sugar-cured ham**

Fold in:

**½ cup mayonnaise or sour cream**

Turn into lightly oiled 1 quart ring mold. Chill until firm. Unmold on crisp salad greens. Serve plain or fill center with cole slaw, potato salad, or assorted relishes.

## HAM-TOMATO ASPIC

10 servings

This is excellent for covered dish functions, and ladies' get-togethers.

Combine:

**2 envelopes unflavored gelatin**
**½ cup cold water**

Mix and bring to a boil:

**3 cups V-8 juice**
**½ teaspoon salt (omit if ham is salty)**
**1 tablespoon grated onion**
**2 tablespoons vinegar**
**1 teaspoon mixed pickling spices pinch red pepper**
**1 teaspoon sugar**

Add gelatin to this mixture, strain and add:

**1 cup ground cooked ham**

Pour in a mold and chill. Serve on lettuce with a dab of salad dressing.

# SPINACH AND HAM SALAD

4 to 6 servings

Use your imagination with this salad. For variation try a little lettuce mixed in for a contrast in color and taste. Add pickled beets, cherry tomatoes, and your favorite cheese cut into Julienne strips. And just for fun, serve your salad in an unusual container—a wooden bread tray will catch your guest's eye.

Wash and drain:

**1 ten ounce package fresh spinach**

Slice into rings:

**1 red onion**

Cut into strips:

**¼ pound Country ham**

Toss lightly with spinach. Make dressing to be poured over salad at the very last minute; mix:

**½ cup vinegar**
**1 cup salad oil**
**6 tablespoons sugar or less, to taste**
**1 teaspoon celery seed**
**salt and pepper to taste**

Garnish with:

**2 sliced hard cooked eggs**
**seasoned croutons (optional)**

# SALMAGUNDI

8 servings

Salmagundi is an old English term which describes our modern-day chef's salad. There are as many ways of preparing this dish as there are ingredients that may go into it. The following is my version of this age-old dish which can be used as a main course for a light lunch or supper.

Arrange the following ingredients on a large serving platter for a beautiful centerpiece that will be served, or arrange ingredients on individual salad plates:

**4 quarts mixed salad greens, such as medium heads of lettuce, fresh spinach and endive**

Distribute evenly over the top of the greens:

**½ pound cheese (Gruyere, Swiss, or Cheddar) thinly sliced into strips**
**1 large Bermuda onion cut into rings**
**4 tomatoes, quartered**
**4 stalks celery, chopped**
**½ pound cooked chicken or turkey sliced in thin strips**
**1 cup crumbled cooked bacon**
**½ pound cooked ham thinly sliced into strips**
**4 hard cooked eggs, sliced**
**16 small sweet pickles**
**1 cup thinly sliced radishes**

Serve with your favorite oil and vinegar dressing.

# HAM DRESSING FOR GREEN SALADS

Makes 1¼ cups

In a small bowl combine:

**½ cup sour cream**
**½ cup mayonnaise**
**1 clove garlic, peeled and slightly crushed**

Refrigerate in a covered jar for 1 hour. Remove garlic and discard it. Add:

**½ cup ground cooked ham**
**1 teaspoon minced onion**
**dash oregano**
**¼ teaspoon freshly ground black pepper**
**½ teaspoon lemon juice**
**dash Worcestershire sauce**

Serve on chilled lettuce or favorite greens with tomatoes.

Ham dishes suitable for a light meal are displayed on the breakfast table in the home of Mr. and Mrs. Richard L. Turner of New Towne Haven. Robyn Monet Harrell waves to her sister Cheri Renee through the bay window. The view reveals a customs house built around the 1640s but not used as a medium through which goods from the Old World were inspected and received into the New World until around 1676.

New Towne Haven is a plantation on the Brewers Creek in Isle of Wight County, Virginia. It was an original land grant of 550 acres by the King on the 14th of February, 1637, made through his Governor of Council of State, Sir John Harvey, to Robert Pitt, merchant, for his "personal adventure and for the transportation of 10 men to the colonies."

# LIGHT MEALS

Light meals consist of breakfast, brunch, lunch, or supper. These innovative ham dishes can be an inspiration for your next party. For consideration of the hostess these dishes can be made ahead. Here are some suggestions.

## SATURDAY MORNING
## GUEST BREAKFAST

*Orange Juice*
*Ham Imperial*
*Fried Apples*
*Buttered Toast*
*Strawberry Preserves*

## SUNDAY MORNING
## BRUNCH

*Bloody Marys*
*Winborne's Buffet Soufflé*
*Sausage Links*
*Fruit and Melon Parfait*
*Cobblestone Coffee Cake*

## BRIDGE LUNCHEON

*Ham Luncheon Quiche*
*Individual Pickled Peach Molds*
*Sweet Potato Pudding*

## MIDNIGHT BREAKFAST

*Party Ham and Artichoke Roll-ups*
*Cheese Soufflé*
*Grand Marnier Fruit Compote*
*Grandma Preece's Buttermilk Biscuits*

## HAM AND ARTICHOKE BRUNCH

8 servings

This is great for special occasions as it is elegant! Serve with *Fried Apples* and sweet rolls or *Cobblestone Coffee Cake.*

Preheat oven to 400°. In a buttered casserole, put a layer of each in the following order:

>    2 **ten ounce packages frozen artichoke hearts, cooked**
>    ½ **pound Smithfield or Country ham, sliced**
>    10 **hard cooked eggs, quartered**
>    1 **pound mushrooms, sauteed in butter**

Combine and pour all over dish:

>    2 **ten ounce cans cream of mushroom soup**
>    2 **tablespoons chopped onions**
>    ¼ **cup cooking sherry**
>    ¼ **teaspoon salt**
>    ¼ **teaspoon garlic salt**
>    ½ **cup grated Cheddar cheese dash Tabasco to taste**

Sprinkle over casserole:

>    ½ **cup grated Cheddar cheese**
>    ¼ **cup bacon bits (optional)**

Bake for 25 to 30 minutes.

## HAM WESLEY WITH PINEAPPLE

8 servings

This is a tasty treat to serve with *Summer Cucumber Mold* or *Lemon Vegetable Salad* for a complete lunch. It is also good prepared for brunch or a coffee.

Preheat oven to 425°. Mix:

>    2 **tablespoons mayonnaise**
>    1 **eight ounce package cream cheese**
>    1 **eight ounce can crushed pineapple, well drained**

Open:

>    2 **eight ounce cans refrigerator crescent rolls**

Flatten each triangle as much as possible. Layer on each triangle one of the following, cut to fit:

>    8 **thin slices cooked Country ham**

Ice the ham with the cream cheese mixture. Or use minced ham, sprinkling it over the cream cheese. Roll up jelly-roll fashion, pinching ends together so mixture does not come out. Secure with toothpicks. Place on an ungreased baking sheet and bake for 18 to 20 minutes. Remove from oven, ice with a little remaining cream cheese mixture, and serve at once.

# VIRGINIA BAKED EGGS BOLT

6 servings

This can be done ahead of time and baked just before serving...nice when you have guests for breakfast.

Preheat oven to 375°. Arrange in layers in a 1½ quart casserole dish or individual ramekins:

**1 cup finely chopped cooked Virginia or Country ham**
**6 hard cooked eggs, sliced**

Top with *Cheese Sauce Bolt.* Sprinkle lightly with:

**3 tablespoons bread crumbs**
**½ cup grated Swiss cheese or 1 slice for each ramekin**
**paprika**

Bake for 8 to 10 minutes for individual ramekins or 12 to 15 minutes for a large casserole dish. Cheese should be golden brown and sauce should be bubbly.

# CHEESE SAUCE BOLT

Melt in a saucepan over low heat:

**4 tablespoons butter**

Stir in:

**1 small onion, grated, or 1 teaspoon onion juice**

Stir in until well blended:

**4 tablespoons flour**

Remove from heat and slowly stir in:

**1 ten ounce can chicken broth**
**5 ounces milk**
**¼ teaspoon salt**
**½ cup grated Swiss cheese**

Return to heat and simmer, stirring continuously until sauce thickens. It is then ready to pour over your ham and egg casserole.

# CREAMED HAM ON TOAST

4 servings

In a saucepan, melt over medium heat:

**4 tablespoons butter**

Sauté:

**2 tablespoons chopped green pepper (optional)**
**1 four ounce can chopped mushrooms (optional)**

Stir in:

**4 tablespoons flour**
**dash salt (omit if ham is salty)**

Blend in:

**2 cups milk**

Cook and stir until thick and bubbly. Stir in and heat through:

**1½ cups minced cooked ham**

Serve over toast or waffles. Garnish with:

**red pimiento strips**

# CREAMED EGGS AND HAM COOLEY

6 servings

Nice for a wedding breakfast. Serve *Fruit and Melon Parfait* as a first course.

Hard cook, shell and slice:

**6 eggs**

Melt in top of double boiler over direct heat:

**¼ cup margarine**

Add and cook until tender:

**1 tablespoon minced onion**

Remove from heat and stir in:

**¼ cup flour**
**½ teaspoon salt (omit if ham is salty)**
**⅛ teaspoon pepper**
**½ teaspoon Worcestershire sauce**

Slowly stir in and cook over boiling water, stirring occasionally until thickened:

**2 cups milk**

Gently stir in the sliced eggs and:

**1 tablespoon minced parsley**
**1½ cups diced cooked ham**

Heat through and serve in individual pastry shells or on toast.

# VIRGINIA HAM BREAKFAST CREPES

4 servings

This recipe makes 12 thin pancakes that may also be stuffed with equal portions of grated Swiss cheese and chopped chicken. Roll crepes, place in a baking dish, and bake at 325° 15 minutes or until cheese melts. Dab with sour cream and serve for brunch or supper.

In medium bowl, beat until fluffy:

**3 eggs**

Add:

**2 tablespoons melted shortening**
**1 cup milk**

Sift into liquid:

**1 cup flour**
**1 teaspoon baking powder**
**1 tablespoon sugar**
**½ cup minced cooked Virginia or Country ham**

Blend well. Pour 1 large mixing spoon of batter into a lightly greased 7 inch crepe pan or skillet. Cook on medium heat, rotating the pan until batter covers the bottom. Cook until bubbles begin to break. Turn and brown the other side. Remove to plates; serve with syrup or blueberry sauce.

# SCRAMBLED EGGS WITH HAM

4 servings

Beat in a bowl:

**6 eggs**
**¼ cup milk**
**dash salt**
**dash pepper**

**½ cup minced or chopped ham**
**½ cup grated Cheddar cheese**
**(optional)**

Pour mixture into heated skillet containing:

**2 tablespoons melted butter**

Scramble until soft and set. Serve.


# HAM OMELET

1 serving

Beat in a bowl:

**2 eggs**

Heat 7 or 8 inch omelet pan or skillet on medium heat. Add:

**1 tablespoon butter**

When butter melts and bubbles, pour eggs into pan. Let cook for a few sec-onds, then lift edges of omelet so that the remaining raw egg can run into the hot pan. Cook until set; scatter over it:

**¼ cup chopped ham**
**¼ cup grated Cheddar or Gruyere cheese (optional)**

Fold over and tilt out of pan onto plate. Serve at once.


# OVEN HAM-FRENCH TOAST

2 servings

Preheat oven to 450°. Combine:

**2 eggs, well beaten**
**¼ cup milk**
**¼ teaspoon cinnamon**
**1 teaspoon vanilla**

Dip into mixture, then place in greased casserole dish:

**2 slices bread**

Top with:

**2 slices ham or ½ cup ground or minced ham**

Dip into egg mixture:

**2 slices bread**

Layer over ham slices. Pour the remaining liquid, if any, over toast and bake for about 15 to 20 minutes. Serve hot with syrup.

# HAM PANCAKE SQUARES

4 to 6 servings

This is a hearty breakfast version of easy pancakes.

Preheat oven to 450°. Combine in a bowl and beat until smooth:

**1 egg**
**2 tablespoons salad oil or melted shortening**

**1 cup milk**
**1 cup packaged pancake mix**
**½ to ¾ cup ham bits**

Pour into a greased 8 by 12 inch dish. Bake 20 minutes. Cut into squares and serve hot with butter and your favorite syrup. Top with fresh blueberries for an extra special treat.

# HAM IMPERIAL

6 servings

An easy favorite treat of all who have been served breakfast at the Harrell beach cottage by the man of the house. Served with *Fried Apples*, this makes a nice brunch.

Preheat oven to 350°. Slightly beat:

**6 eggs**

Add:

**4 slices white bread, cut or torn into small bits**
**½ cup milk**
**1 cup ground or chopped cooked ham**

**2 heaping tablespoons mayonnaise**
**dash Worcestershire sauce**
**½ cup chopped green peppers (optional)**

Mix well until bread is dissolved and mixture is thoroughly blended. Pour into well buttered fry pan, casserole dish, or in individual casserole dishes. Place in preheated oven for 20 minutes or until center is firm. Slices of cheese may be added just before removing from oven if *Ham Imperial au Gratin* is desired. Serve with tomato slices or wedges to add color.

# CHEESE, EGGS, AND HAM

You can serve as many as you like with this quick dish.

Preheat oven to 450°. Line a greased shallow baking dish or individual casseroles with the desired number of slices of:

**Country ham**

Layer on top of each slice of ham a slice of:

**Swiss cheese**

Break on top of cheese and ham the

desired number of:

**eggs**

Sprinkle with:

**dash pepper**

Pour over egg whites until yellows just peep through:

**cream**

Bake for 10 minutes, then sprinkle with:

**Parmesan cheese**

Continue to bake 10 minutes longer. Garnish with parsley and serve at once. Tomato wedges add a splash of color.

---

## HAM AND EGGS BENEDICT

---

2 servings

Prepare hollandaise sauce; in top of double boiler slightly beat:

**2 egg yolks**

Slowly stir in:

**¼ cup butter**

Gradually add by spoonfuls, beating after each addition:

**¼ cup boiling water**

Cook until just thickened, stirring constantly. Do not let hot water in bottom of double boiler touch the top pan. Remove pan from heat and add:

**1½ tablespoons lemon juice**
**dash cayenne**

**about ¼ teaspoon salt**

Cover and keep warm in top of double boiler. Slice in half, butter, and toast:

**2 English muffins**

Arrange on each half one of:

**4 ham slices**

Top each ham slice with one of:

**4 poached eggs**

Top with hollandaise sauce. Garnish with a sprinkle of:

**cayenne**
**chopped parsley**

*Cheddar Cheese Sauce* can be used instead of the hollandaise sauce.

---

## CHEDDAR CHEESE SAUCE

---

Melt on low heat:

**2 tablespoons butter**

Add:

**2 tablespoons flour**

Stir in gradually and continue stirring

until thickened:

**1 cup milk**

Add and stir until melted:

**1 cup grated or chunked sharp Cheddar cheese**

# QUICK EGGS BENEDICT

4 servings

Split, butter, and toast:

**2 English muffins**

On each muffin half place one of:

**4 slices Virginia ham**

Fry:

**4 eggs**

Place eggs on top of ham. Heat:

**1 ten ounce can undiluted Cheddar cheese soup**

Spoon desired amount over each muffin. Garnish with paprika. For lunch or supper, serve with broccoli spears.

# SWISS CHEESE AND HAM OVEN OMELET

4 servings

Preheat oven to 350°. Melt in a saucepan:

**2 tablespoons butter**

Add:

**¼ cup finely chopped onion**

Fry until golden. Combine:

**4 eggs, well beaten**
**½ cup milk**

**⅛ teaspoon pepper**
**½ cup minced cooked ham**

Add the onion and stir well. Pour into greased 1 quart casserole. Cut in strips:

**4 ounces Swiss cheese**

Top casserole with cheese strips, which will sink into the egg mixture. Bake 40 minutes until puffed high, then serve at once. You can easily double this recipe; use a 1½ quart mold to make 8 servings.

# EGGS BAKED IN HAM RINGS

1 serving

Increase the ingredients to accommodate the number of people you wish to serve. If you do not have slices of ham, chop or grind bits of ham and press into the bottom and around the sides of muffin tins, then continue with the recipe.

Preheat oven to 325°. Grease the bottoms of muffin tins, cut to fit depth of tin, and line the sides with:

**1 slice cooked ham**

Drop into the muffin cup:

**1 egg**

Pour over the egg:

**½ teaspoon melted butter**

Sprinkle with:

**dash salt**
**dash pepper**
**dash paprika**

Bake for about 10 minutes until egg is set. Turn out onto:

**1 slice pineapple**

# EGGS IN A NEST

4 servings

A new look for ham and eggs, but with the familiar delicious flavor. This makes a nice breakfast treat for guests.

Preheat oven to 350°. Split and butter:

**2 English muffins**

Separate from yolks and beat until soft peaks form:

**4 egg whites**

Layer on each split muffin one of:

**4 slices Country ham**

Ice ham with whipped egg whites, forming a nest. Make a cavity in each nest and slip into each one of:

**4 egg yolks**

Bake 10 minutes, until eggs are set. Garnish with:

**4 sprigs parsley**

Serve with fresh fruit or juice for a complete meal.

# WINBORNE'S BUFFET SOUFFLE

4 servings

A true soufflé is made from a basic white sauce with separated well beaten egg yolks and whites folded into the mixture. This is an easy version of that ancient dish; it offers the same guest appeal, but holds its shape over a long period of time.

Alternate in layers in a buttered casserole:

**5 slices buttered bread, cubed**
**¾ pound grated sharp cheese**

**½ cup minced cooked ham**

Beat until light and fluffy:

**4 eggs**

Add:

**2 cups milk**
**1 teaspoon dry mustard**
  **dash salt (omit if ham is salty)**
  **dash cayenne**

Stir and pour over bread and cheese mixture. Let stand in refrigerator overnight or several hours before baking. Bake 1 hour in preheated 350° oven.

# HAM AND SPINACH SOUFFLE

4 servings

Preheat oven to 350°. Soak until soft:

**4 slices white bread**
**about 1 cup milk**

Combine in a saucepan with:

**3 tablespoons melted butter**
**1 small onion, grated or finely minced**

Cook until smooth, over medium heat, stirring constantly. A wire whisk is helpful in making a smooth sauce. Add and stir well:

**1 cup finely chopped, cooked, well-drained spinach**

**½ to ¾ cup ground cooked ham**
**3 well beaten egg yolks**

Season with:

**dash salt (omit if ham is salty)**
**dash pepper**
**dash ground nutmeg**

Beat until stiff:

**3 egg whites**
**dash cream of tartar**

Gently fold egg whites into the mixture and turn into a generously buttered soufflé dish. Place in a pan of hot water and bake for 45 to 50 minutes. Serve immediately with a hollandaise, tomato sauce, or cheese sauce.

# HAM AND CHEESE SOUFFLE

8 servings

This is a marvelous old family recipe that was given to me by a former home economics student of mine, Kit Webb. When served with *Pink Cranberry Freeze* and *Grandmama Jones' Hot Rolls,* it makes an elegant luncheon. A soufflé must be served immediately upon removal from the oven.

Preheat oven to 350°. In a saucepan melt:

**6 tablespoons butter**

Stir in until well-blended:

**6 tablespoons flour**
**¾ teaspoon salt (omit if ham is salty)**

**⅛ teaspoon pepper**
**¼ teaspoon dry mustard**
**⅛ teaspoon nutmeg**

Add gradually and stir while cooking over medium heat until mixture thickens and bubbles:

**1½ cups milk**

Remove from heat. Beat in a separate bowl:

**6 egg yolks**

Beat cooked mixture slowly into egg yolks. Beat in:

**about 1 cup minced cooked ham**
**1½ to 2 cups shredded sharp cheese**
**3 tablespoons grated Parmesan cheese**

Beat in separate bowl until stiff but not dry:

**6 egg whites**

**¼ teaspoon cream of tartar**

Gently fold cheese and ham mixture into egg whites. Pour mixture into ungreased 8 inch soufflé dish. Bake 55 minutes or until puffed, golden and firm to touch. Serve immediately. Reduce proportions by half for a 6 inch soufflé dish.

Ham dishes displayed with antique kitchen equipment: a sausage grinder and corn sheller, a German soup kettle and ladle, and a wooden dough bowl.

LIGHT MEALS

## LUNCHEON QUICHE

12 servings

Quiche is the French word for pie or tart. The classic Quiche Lorraine originated in Alsace, Lorraine. The addition of ham to a quiche turns a provincial dish into a gourmet delight and a complete meal. A light white wine is recommended.

Prepare enough pastry dough to line a quiche pan or 10 inch deep dish pie pan; flute edges of pastry and set in refrigerator while mixing filling. You may use 2 fresh or frozen deep dish pie shells; distribute ingredients evenly between them. Preheat oven to 450°. Beat until light and fluffy:

**3 eggs**

Add:

**1½ cups half and half**
**½ teaspoon white pepper**
**½ teaspoon salt (omit if ham is salty)**
**dash ground nutmeg**
**dash cayenne**

Sprinkle over bottom of pie crust:

**1 cup chopped ham**
**1½ cups shredded Swiss cheese**

Carefully pour egg mixture into the pan; place pan in oven and bake for 12 minutes. Reduce heat to 325° and bake an additional 20 to 25 minutes, until custard is set and the crust and filling are lightly browned. Cut in wedges and serve while hot.

## HAM AND ONION QUICHE

12 servings

Prepare unbaked pie shell:

**9 inch deep dish pie shell**

You may also use 2 regular pie shells, in which case distribute ingredients between them. Preheat oven to 350°. Cover pie shell with:

**½ cup minced or chopped ham**
**½ cup grated Swiss cheese**

Beat until frothy:

**4 eggs**

Add:

**1½ cups light cream or half and half**
**1⅜ ounces packaged onion soup mix**

Beat well and pour over ham and cheese in shell. Bake 45 to 50 minutes or until custard is well set and lightly browned on top. Cool and serve.

# HAM-ASPARAGUS QUICHE

6 servings

This quiche is a favorite version of Edna Brooks Turner, whose breakfast room introduces this chapter.

Prepare pastry for:

**9 inch deep dish pie crust**

Preheat oven to 400°. Sprinkle on bottom of pastry shell:

**2 ten ounce packages frozen asparagus, cooked, drained, chopped**
**¾ cup chopped cooked Country ham**
**½ pound Gouda cheese, diced**
**1 four ounce can chopped mushrooms, drained**

Mix:

**4 eggs, beaten**
**1½ cups half and half or heavy cream**
**⅛ teaspoon nutmeg**
**dash pepper**

Pour eggs over the mixture in the pastry shell. Bake 10 minutes; reduce heat to 375° and cook for 40 minutes or until done. For a variation, use 2 ten ounce packages frozen chopped broccoli or spinach instead of asparagus.

# HAM AND CHEESE PIE

6 servings

Prepare:

**9 inch pie crust, unbaked**

Preheat oven to 350°. Layer in crust:

**4 slices Swiss cheese**
**4 thin slices cooked Country ham**

Combine:

**2 eggs, well beaten**
**8 ounces sour cream**

Pour over pie. Bake for 35 to 40 minutes until golden brown. This cuts like a custard pie.

# "HAMMY PIE"

6 servings

Prepare:

**9 inch pie shell, unbaked**

Preheat oven to 350°. Mix well:

**1 pound cooked smoked ham or ½ pound cooked Country ham, chopped**
**2 eggs, slightly beaten**
**½ cup grated onion**
**¼ cup prepared mustard**
**¼ cup ketchup**
**1 tablespoon parsley flakes**
**1 tablespoon Worcestershire sauce**
**¼ teaspoon garlic salt**
**1 cup dry bread crumbs**

Spread in pie shell and bake for 20 to 30 minutes. Remove from oven and arrange on top of pie:

**3 slices American cheese, halved**

Return to oven just to melt cheese.

# HAM PIZZA

8 servings

Preheat oven to 375°. Open and separate into sections:

**1 eight ounce can refrigerator crescent rolls**

Flatten out rolls and place in a semicircle as close together as possible on a cookie sheet. Mix well:

**1 eight ounce can tomato sauce**
**½ teaspoon Italian seasoning**

**¼ cup ketchup**

Spread half of mixture on crescent rolls. Sprinkle over this:

**¼ to ½ cup ground cooked ham**

Spread remaining mixture over ham and top with:

**1 eight ounce package grated Mozzarella cheese**

Bake for 15 to 20 minutes. Serve at once.

---

# HAM AND CHEESE STRATA

6 to 8 servings

Trim crust from:

**10 slices bread**

Arrange 5 slices on the bottom of a buttered baking dish and layer:

**½ cup ground cooked ham**
**4 ounces American or Cheddar cheese**

Cover with remaining 5 slices of bread and repeat layers of:

**½ cup ground cooked ham**
**4 ounces American or Cheddar cheese**

Mix:

**3 eggs, slightly beaten**
**2¾ cups milk**
**½ teaspoon dry mustard**

Pour over layers in casserole dish and cover. Refrigerate overnight. Bake for 1 hour at 350°. Slice in squares and serve.

---

# HAM AND CHEESE PUDDING

6 servings

Preheat oven to 325°. Trim off and discard crusts of bread and cut each slice into quarters. Arrange in a shallow casserole dish:

**6 slices day old bread**

Sprinkle over bread:

**½ cup minced ham**

Sauté until golden:

**2 tablespoons butter**
**¾ cup minced onion**

Pour over ham. Beat lightly:

**4 eggs**

Stir in:

**¾ cup grated Cheddar cheese**
**3 cups milk**

**½ teaspoon nutmeg**
**dash salt and pepper**

Pour mixture over bread and ham. Place dish in a large pan containing 2 cups of water. Bake 45 minutes or until firm.

## HAM AND NOODLES

4 servings

In a saucepan, brown:

**1½ cups cubed cooked ham**
**1 four ounce can sliced mushrooms, drained**
**2 tablespoons butter or margarine**

Stir in:

**¾ cup milk**
**1 tablespoon sherry (optional)**
**2 cups cooked noodles**
**¼ cup grated Parmesan cheese**

Continue cooking until ingredients are well blended. Garnish with:

**chopped parsley**

## WELSH RAREBIT WITH VIRGINIA HAM

4 servings

This is a good dish for a luncheon because it takes a minimum amount of effort and time. Serve with a refreshing dessert, such as *Strawberry Bavarian Marcelle.*

Split and toast:

**4 English muffins**

Slightly broil:

**4 slices cooked Virginia or Country ham**

Melt:

**2 tablespoons butter**

Brown in the butter:

**8 slices pineapple**

Make *Cheddar Cheese Sauce* or heat, according to package directions:

**1 ten ounce package frozen Welsh rarebit sauce**

Top toasted muffins with ham, sliced pineapple, and sauce. Serve immediately.

# HAM CORNUCOPIAS

12 servings

A Tidewater artist, Jim Pittman, gave me his favorite way to use ham. For a busy bachelor, easy dishes are a must. Serve for lunch with *French Bread*.

Remove carefully any pieces of shell or cartilage from:

**1 pound crabmeat**

In a mixing bowl combine and mix thoroughly with the crabmeat:

**½ cup mayonnaise**
**2 hard cooked eggs, finely chopped**
**1 teaspoon Worcestershire sauce**

**2 tablespoons lemon juice**
**2 tablespoons finely chopped parsley**
**dash salt**
**dash pepper**
**¼ cup diced black olives (optional)**

Distribute mixture among:

**12 slices Country or sugar-cured ham**

Roll each slice into a cone shape. Serve on lettuce or watercress. Make bite-size cones with small pieces of ham for appetizers or for cocktails.

# HAM-ASPARAGUS ROLL-UPS

4 servings

Serve with *Frozen Fruit Salad* and *Edna's Hot Rolls* for a quick, elegant lunch. Prepare:

**16 asparagus spears**
**8 slices cooked ham**

Wrap a slice of ham around 2 asparagus spears and secure with a toothpick. Repeat for all the slices of ham. Place roll-ups on a broiler pan and top each one with one of:

**8 slices Mozzarella or Cheddar cheese**

Broil until cheese melts and serve immediately.

# PARTY HAM AND ARTICHOKE ROLL-UPS

6 to 12 servings

Great for a midnight breakfast, these can be made ahead then baked just before serving.

Preheat oven to 350°. Make a white sauce; melt in a saucepan:

**4 tablespoons butter**

Stir in:

**4 tablespoons flour**

Remove from heat and stir in:

**2 cups milk**

When smooth, return to heat and stir constantly until thick. Add and blend well:

**⅛ teaspoon seasoned salt**
**⅛ teaspoon cayenne pepper**
**¼ teaspoon ground nutmeg**
  **dash paprika**
  **pinch white pepper**

Stir in and blend over low heat until cheese melts:

**¼ to ½ cup grated Swiss cheese**
**¼ to ½ cup grated Parmesan cheese**

Remove from heat and add:

**3 tablespoons sherry**

Prepare according to package directions:

**2 ten ounce packages frozen or 2 one pound cans artichoke hearts**

Place one artichoke on each of:

**12 thin slices Country ham**

If artichoke is large, cut in half before placing on ham. Roll up and place in a buttered casserole dish, letting sides touch. Pour prepared sauce over roll-ups. Combine:

**¾ cup buttered bread crumbs**
**¼ to ½ cup grated Swiss cheese**
**¼ to ½ cup grated Parmesan cheese**

Sprinkle crumb-cheese mixture over casserole and bake for 25 to 30 minutes. This dish may be made ahead and baked just before serving.

---

## HAM AND OLIVE MOUSSE

---

24 servings

Mary Ann Eure prepares this ham mousse to accompany a cold buffet. It is also an excellent salad for luncheons... something a little different.

Line a lightly oiled 1½ quart mold with enough to decorate mold:

**about ½ cup sliced olives**

Dissolve in a large mixing bowl:

**1 three ounce package lemon gelatin**
**1 cup boiling water**

Add and stir until blended:

**1 eight ounce package softened cream cheese**

Continue to add:

**1 ten ounce can tomato soup**
**1 to 1½ cups ground cooked ham**
**1 tablespoon grated horseradish**
**½ cup chopped olives**
**¼ cup chopped celery**
**½ cup mayonnaise**
**½ teaspoon salt (omit if ham is salty)**

Mix lightly and pour into prepared mold. Chill until firm. Unmold on crisp lettuce, and serve with pumpernickel bread or rice crackers.

# HAM CHARLOTTE

4 servings

This delicious dish takes ten minutes to prepare.

Combine in a saucepan over low heat until melted:

> **1 cup shredded Cheddar cheese**
> **1 cup mayonnaise**
> **½ cup milk**

Place on each of 4 plates one of:

**4 slices bread, preferably rye**

Top each slice of bread with 1 of:

**4 slices Country ham**

Open and drain:

> **1 twelve ounce can asparagus spears**

Top each ham slice with 2 asparagus spears. Spoon 3 to 4 tablespoons of sauce over each plate. Garnish with apple rings for color.

# ROCHAMBEAU

6 servings

Martha Sieg, my home economics professor at Madison College, shared this favorite ham recipe with us.

Toast:

> **6 slices bread**

Place one of each of the following on each slice of toast:

> **6 slices cooked ham**
> **6 slices cooked chicken or turkey**

Cover with *Sauce Paulette.*

# SAUCE PAULETTE

Melt in a saucepan:

> **1 tablespoon butter**

Add and cook for 1 minute:

> **1 tablespoon flour**

Stir in:

> **2 cups chicken or turkey broth or bouillon**

Add and stir until well blended:

> **½ teaspoon salt**
> **1 teaspoon pepper**
> **3 sprigs parsley**

Bring to a boil. Lower heat and simmer for 30 minutes. Discard parsley. Remove sauce from heat and blend in:

> **2 egg yolks, beaten**

Add:

> **juice of 1 lemon**
> **1 teaspoon finely chopped parsley**
> **1 four ounce can mushrooms, drained**
> **1 tablespoon butter**

This sauce freezes beautifully; reheat over a double boiler. It also goes well with salmon casseroles.

# HAM A LA KING

6 servings

Serve with *Laura's Fruit Salad* for a complete meal.

Sauté for about 5 minutes:

**¼ cup butter**
**3 tablespoons chopped green pepper**
**1½ tablespoons chopped pimiento**

Add and cook for 1 minute longer:

**½ cup sliced mushrooms**

Remove vegetables from the pan and reserve. Use liquid in pan to dissolve:

**1½ tablespoons flour**

Gradually stir in:

**1½ cups light cream**

Cook until smooth and thick, stirring constantly. Add the reserved vegetables to the cream sauce with:

**2 cups diced cooked ham, fat removed**

Season with:

**dash paprika**
**½ teaspoon salt (omit if ham is salty)**

Cook over low heat for 2 minutes, stirring constantly. Beat slightly:

**2 egg yolks**

Stir some of sauce into the eggs, blending well; stir egg mixture into remaining hot sauce. Cook 1 minute longer. Remove from heat and stir in, if desired:

**2 tablespoons sherry (optional)**

Serve on rice, noodles, toast or heated patty shells. For variety, substitute for ham a 1 pound can of drained, flaked red salmon or 4 quartered hard cooked eggs or 1 pound cooked shrimp.

# SLICED HAM WITH RAISINS

4 servings

Mix sauce:

**6 tablespoons brown sugar**
**½ teaspoon vinegar**
**1 teaspoon mustard**
**1 teaspoon water**

Place in frying pan and fry according to package directions:

**1 pound package uncooked breakfast ham slices**

When almost done, spread with sauce mixture. Top with:

**4 slices pineapple**
**½ cup raisins**

Let sauce bubble, then serve. Slices of cooked ham may also be used; just heat with the sauce and serve. For a full fruity flavor, simmer the raw ham slices in the juice drained from the can of pineapple, add the raisins, and serve.

# GROUND HAM ON PINEAPPLE

4 servings

Preheat oven to 400°. Combine:

**1 cup ground cooked ham**
**1 teaspoon prepared mustard**
**2 tablespoons mayonnaise**

Spread this mixture on:

**4 slices pineapple**

Bake in a greased pan for about 10 minutes. Serve on lettuce.

# HAM-STUFFED EGGS

12 servings

A nice side dish.

Peel and slice:

**6 hard cooked eggs**

Scoop out yellow without breaking whites. Mash and combine with yolk, enough to moisten yolks:

**mayonnaise**

**1 teaspoon mustard**
**⅛ cup minced cooked ham**
**⅛ cup finely minced pickle**
**(optional)**
**dash pepper**

Mix well and stuff back into whites of egg; use fluted tube on pastry bag for a decorative effect.

# BAKED HAM-STUFFED TOMATOES

4 servings

Preheat oven to 350°. Slice off the top half-inch from each of:

**4 medium tomatoes**

Scoop out tomato pulp and mix with:

**6 tablespoons bread crumbs**
**3 tablespoons chopped celery**
**½ cup grated Cheddar cheese**
**1 cup ground cooked ham**
**6 tablespoons melted butter**
**1 teaspoon minced onion**
**(optional)**

Stuff tomatoes with mixture. Sprinkle each with:

**grated Parmesan cheese**

Place tomatoes in a pan with:

**¼ cup water**

Bake for 30 minutes. Half strips of bacon may be laid across the tomatoes when they are nearly done. Place under the broiler until bacon is crisp.

# HAM SAUCE FOR BROCCOLI

Makes 1 cup

Melt in a saucepan:

> **1 tablespoon liquid from cooked broccoli**
> **1 eight ounce package cream cheese**

**¼ cup sour cream**
**½ cup chopped cooked ham**

Place cooked broccoli in serving dish, and pour warm sauce over it.

# HAM STUFFED BAKED POTATOES

6 servings

Scrub, pat dry, grease and wrap in foil:

> **3 large baking potatoes**

Bake in a 400° oven for 1 hour or until tender when squeezed. Melt in a saucepan:

> **2 tablespoons butter**

Stir in and cook until limp:

> **¼ to ½ cup minced onion**
> **1 cup chopped mushrooms, or ½ cup canned chopped mushrooms, drained**

Stir in:

> **¼ cup chopped cooked ham**

Cut each baked potato in half lengthwise; scoop out potato, being careful not to break skins. Place skins in a baking dish. Mash potatoes well; stir in:

> **½ cup sour cream**
> **1 tablespoon butter**
> **1 egg, lightly beaten**
> **½ cup grated Swiss or Cheddar cheese**

Stir in ham mixture. Pile potato stuffing into skins and top with:

> **½ cup grated Swiss or Cheddar cheese**

Bake at 375° for 15 to 20 minutes, until cheese melts and potatoes are heated through. These potatoes can be made ahead and refrigerated or frozen until ready to bake.

For convenience, prepare 10 pounds of potatoes. Actually, it is just as easy to make 10 pounds of potatoes as six potatoes. The following variation is recommended, however, for frozen stuffed potatoes. After baking and scooping out the potato pulp in a bowl, add: 3 cups chopped onions, 1½ to 2 cups chopped ham and the cook gets *no* compliments if she omits 2 tablespoons ham drippings, 1 stick margarine, salt and pepper to taste, 1 pound coarsely grated sharp cheese. Mix with fingers because if whipped, the potatoes turn to a mushy consistency after thawing. Stuff shells, place on a cookie sheet and cover to freeze. When frozen, place in plastic bags. Allow to thaw 1 hour before heating.

# HAMWICHES

## BLENDER HAM SALAD SPREAD

Makes 1½ cups

Put into blender, cover and process at blend setting until smooth:

    **¼ cup mayonnaise**
    **2 whole sweet pickles, diced**

**2 tablespoons chopped onion**
**1 cup diced cooked ham**
**1 hard-cooked egg, diced**
**1 tablespoon pickle juice**

Spread on your favorite bread for a treat!

## MIMI HINES GROUND HAM SANDWICH SPREAD

Makes 3 to 3½ cups

Grind together:

    **2 to 3 cups cooked ham**
    **3 whole sweet cucumber pickles**
    **3 pieces celery**

Moisten, to make a good spreading consistency, with:

    **1½ cups (approx.) mayonnaise**

This is delicious on toasted bread or you can spread it on bread and bake in a sandwich toaster or place under the broiler. This spread will keep several weeks in the refrigerator.

## VIRGINIA HAM SPREAD

Makes 2¼ cups

Mix:

    **1½ cups ground Virginia or Country ham**
    **½ cup chopped pimiento**

    **¼ cup mayonnaise**

Serve on regular sandwich bread or cut bread into fancy bite-size shapes and spread with ham mixture for fancy canapes.

# SUPER SUPPER SANDWICH

4 servings

This makes a whole meal with the addition of a fresh fruit salad or *Holiday Cranberry Mold.*

Spread lightly with mayonnaise, then place in a large well-buttered baking dish:

**4 slices white sandwich bread**

Add in layers:

**4 thin slices Smithfield or Country ham**
**4 slices sharp Cheddar cheese, about ¼ inch thick**
**4 slices chicken or turkey breast**

Spread with mayonnaise and top sandwiches with:

**4 slices bread**

Blend well:

**3 eggs, slightly beaten**
**2 cups milk**
**½ teaspoon salt**
**½ teaspoon dry mustard**

Pour over sandwich; cover and refrigerate overnight or for several hours. When ready to bake, combine:

**1 ten ounce can cream of mushroom soup**
**¼ cup milk**

Pour over sandwiches. Bake uncovered in 350° oven for about 1 hour. About 10 minutes before removing from oven, place on top of each sandwich 2 of:

**8 asparagus tips**

Garnish with:

**chopped pimiento**

# HAMATARIAN SANDWICH

4 servings

Having a table of bridge for a luncheon ....Try this!

Sauté until tender:

**3 tablespoons butter**
**½ cup chopped onion**
**½ cup chopped bell peppers**
**¾ cup sliced mushrooms**

Add:

**12 black olives, sliced**
**dash black pepper**

Split:

**4 poppyseed rolls**

Top each roll with one each of:

**4 slices ham or chopped ham or ham bits**
**4 slices tomato**

Sprinkle with:

**black pepper**

Top tomatoes with sautéed vegetables and:

**4 slices Swiss cheese**

Place under broiler until cheese melts.

# HAM TOMATO DELIGHT

4 servings

Place on a baking sheet or on 4 slices bread:

**3 medium tomatoes, sliced**

Sprinkle each slice with:

**dash oregano**
**dab mayonnaise**

Place on top of each tomato slice one of:

**4 slices ham**
**4 slices cheese**

Broil for 3 minutes or until cheese melts. Asparagus spears and *French Bread* complete the meal. If you are a dieter, omit bread and broil tomato slices with bits or slices of ham and cheese.

# HAM AND PEANUT BUTTER SANDWICH

4 servings

Stretch your imagination and try this one!

Combine:

**½ cup peanut butter**
**¼ cup cooked minced or ground ham**
**¼ cup mayonnaise**

**2 tablespoons pickle relish (optional)**

Spread on:

**8 slices bread**

Cut diagonally and serve, or broil open-faced, then top with slice of bread and broil few minutes longer.

# HAM SANDWICH BEATY

4 to 6 servings

Combine well:

**1 cup diced chicken**
**½ cup halved green grapes**
**½ cup chopped pecans**
**2 hard cooked eggs, finely chopped**
**¼ cup finely chopped celery**
**¼ cup mayonnaise**
**¼ cup salad dressing**

Split open:

**4 to 6 sesame seed rolls**

Top with 1 slice each in layers:

**4 to 6 slices cooked ham**
**4 to 6 slices pineapple**

Spoon onto each about 2 tablespoons of chicken mixture. Serve with chips and wedges of honeydew. This same chicken mixture combined with ½ cup diced ham makes a nice salad to be served on a slice of pineapple on lettuce or in a halved avocado.

# HAM BARBECUE

10 to 12 servings

Mix all of these ingredients in a large bowl:

> ten ounces canned or bottled chili sauce
> 1 teaspoon Worcestershire sauce
> 1 teaspoon vinegar

> about 2 tablespoons sugar, to taste
> 1 teaspoon mustard

Chop and add:

> 2 pounds cooked sugar-cured ham

Mix well and heat in a skillet. Serve on buns.


# HAM AND CHEESE REUBEN

1 serving

Remove crust (if you prefer) from:

> 2 slices rye bread

Put between the two slices:

> 1 slice ham
> 1 slice Swiss cheese
> 1 tablespoon sauerkraut

Spread the sandwich on the outside with:

> soft butter or margarine

Fry until golden brown and crisp. Garnish with pickle and serve with a favorite salad to complete a delightful lunch.


# SAILBOAT HAM BUNS DRAPER

8 servings

This is an attractive meal for a child's party.

Combine:

> 2 cups chopped ham
> ½ cup mayonnaise
> 2 tablespoons minced onion
> 3 tablespoons chopped sweet pickle

Spread this ham mixture on:

> 4 hotdog or submarine buns, halved lengthwise

Halve to form triangles then mount diagonally on toothpicks to form the sails of a boat when inserted in buns:

> 4 squares American cheese

The circa 1700 Hepplewhite table in the
formal dining room of Pembroke is elegantly
laden with a ham entree and accompaniments.
The epergne holding the fresh fruit arrangement dates around 1700 and is made of old
English silver and Waterford crystal.

# ENTREES AND ACCOMPANIMENTS

Ham is often the center of the menu, the meat around which you plan your meal. For centuries, tables in the South have groaned from the weight of tasty hams and those side dishes that go so well with it, such as *Tomato Pudding, Corn Pudding, Snap Beans, Pickled* and *Brandied Peaches, Glazed Sweet Potatoes,* and *Peanut Pie.* Many recipes are family treasures and have been passed from one generation to the next.

Ham has for centuries been traditionally sliced and served with another meat, yet it may be combined with other foods for new and original entrées. The combination of Smithfield ham with crabmeat is a Tidewater, Virginia, favorite. *Ham-Stuffed Crepes* or *Chicken Cordon Bleu* will star at any dinner party. Besides the traditional ways to prepare a whole ham, including the varieties of glazes, many innovative entrées using the leftover pieces and bits of ham as well as accompaniments for a ham dinner are included in this chapter. For a complete dinner serve:

*Curried Chicken and Ham*
*Sweet Potato and Apple Casserole*
*Buttered Garden Peas*
*Summer Cucumber Mold*
*Edna's Hot Rolls*
*Peanut Pie*

## HAM BAKED IN PASTRY

20 to 30 servings

The pastry-wrapped ham is for a festive and gala event. Mardi Gras parties often feature this lovely entrée. A cooked boned and rolled sugar-cured ham would make for easier slicing and serving.

Preheat oven to 425°. Make pie crust by combining in a bowl:

**4½ cups sifted flour**
**1½ cups shortening**
**1½ teaspoons salt**

Work until the consistency of corn meal. Add gradually:

**½ cup ice water**

Knead and begin to form into a ball. Add gradually:

**¼ cup ice water**

Continue kneading and shaping. If you need more water, add 1 tablespoon at a time. Work dough into a ball. Pat flat and roll into a large circle, about ⅛ inch thick.

Dry completely and enclose in pastry, sealing edges:

**1 ten pound sugar-cured ham, cooked**

With extra dough, make decorations if you wish. Place ham on an ungreased baking sheet and brush lightly with a mixture of:

**2 egg yolks**
**2 tablespoons water**

Bake about 30 minutes in middle of oven or until golden brown. When done remove ham to a platter. Let cool before slicing.

## SUNNY HAM-FILLED CREPES

18 to 20 servings

In a mixing bowl, beat only until well blended:

**2 eggs**

Add:

**1 cup milk**
**½ teaspoon salt**
**1 cup all purpose flour**

Stir until smooth. Cover and let stand at least half an hour. The batter should be thin, just thick enough to coat a spoon when dipped in it. If the batter is too thick, stir in a little more milk. Heat a 5 or 6 inch crepe pan or skillet and grease lightly with:

**1 teaspoon salad oil**

Pour in just enough batter to cover the pan with a very thin layer. Tilt the pan so that the batter spreads evenly. If there is a little too much, tip the pan over the mixing bowl and pour the extra back. Non-stick pans are excellent and do not require oiling. Cook on one side until batter is set and pancake can be easily turned with a spatula and browned on the other side. Cook pancakes one by one. Stack neatly. Keep warm if serving immediately, or set aside and reheat later in the oven. These crepes freeze very well for future use. Just thaw, then heat when ready to eat. Fill with *Sunny Ham Filling.*

# SUNNY HAM FILLING

Bring to a boil in a saucepan:

**3 cups water**
**dash salt**

Cook according to package directions:

**2 ten ounce packages frozen**
**chopped spinach**

Drain spinach thoroughly and combine until mixed completely with:

**1 eight ounce package**
**cream cheese**

Brown in a frying pan:

**1 cup chopped cooked ham**
**½ cup chopped onions**

Add to spinach mixture and blend well. Fill *Sunny Ham-Filled Crepes* and fold over. Top each crepe with:

**dab sour cream**
**grated Parmesan cheese**

# CHICKEN CORDON BLEU

8 servings

This recipe was given to me by Mrs. Bathurst Daingerfield Peachy, Jr., who was a hostess at Colonial Williamsburg for many years.

Bone, skin, and halve:

**4 whole chicken breasts**

Layer one slice of each, then roll to form 8 rolls:

**8 slices Country ham**
**8 slices Swiss cheese**

Roll a boned chicken breast half around each ham and cheese roll. Season each with just a sprinkle of:

**salt**
**pepper**

Roll each in:

**½ cup flour**

Dip each in:

**4 eggs, beaten**

Roll in a mixture of:

**1 cup fine bread crumbs**
**10 tablespoons sesame seeds**

Dip again in egg mixture then in crumbs. The chicken rolls may be prepared ahead of time up to this point and refrigerated until serving time. Brown gently in a mixture of:

**3 tablespoons salad oil**
**2 tablespoons butter**

Turn the rolled chicken breasts 3 times during browning. Cook until tender, about 15 minutes. Near the end of the cooking time add:

**3 tablespoons minced onion**

Remove chicken and drain on paper towels. Keep chicken warm in a low oven while making the sauce. To pan drippings add:

**1 cup sliced fresh mushrooms or**
**1 four ounce can sliced**
**mushrooms, drained**
**3 to 4 ounces dry white wine**
**2 tablespoons beef extract**

1 tablespoon Worcestershire
   sauce
½ teaspoon Tabasco
1 pint sour cream

Simmer until sauce is reduced by one-third. Pour sauce over chicken on a warm platter and serve.

## CHICKEN CORDON BLEU CASSEROLE

8 servings

For an elegant dinner, try this!

Preheat oven to 350°.

Skin, bone, halve, and flatten:
   **4 chicken breasts**

Mix well:
   **1 egg**
   **1 tablespoon water**

Dip chicken in egg mixture then dip in:
   **¾ cup bread crumbs**

Dip again in egg mixture and crumbs, then dip in:
   **¼ cup sesame seeds**

Brown breasts on all sides in a skillet in a mixture of:
   **¼ cup cooking oil**
   **4 tablespoons butter**

Drain on paper towel. Layer on each chicken breast one of:

   **8 slices Country ham**
   **8 slices Mozzarella or Swiss cheese**

Roll up breasts and place in a casserole dish. Sauté in remaining oil and butter:
   **½ to 1 pound mushrooms, chopped**

Pour mushrooms over chicken. Bring just to boiling and pour over chicken and mushrooms:
   **¾ cup white wine**

To this point recipe may be made ahead of time and refrigerated. Just before serving time preheat oven to 350° and bring to boiling:
   **8 ounces whipping cream**

Pour over chicken. Place baking dish in oven for about 25 to 30 minutes. Chicken is done when it springs back to the touch.

## QUICK CORDON BLEU

6 servings

Skin, bone, halve, and flatten:
   **3 chicken breasts**

Top flattened breast with one each of the following, cut to fit:
   **6 slices Swiss cheese**
   **6 slices Country ham**

Roll up each breast and secure with

toothpicks. Brown in:
   **2 tablespoons butter**

Stir in:
   **1 ten ounce can cream of mushroom soup**
   **¼ cup milk or light cream or white wine**

Cover; cook over low heat for 25

minutes or until tender, stirring occasionally. Garnish with:

**chopped parsley**
**paprika**

## CURRIED CHICKEN AND HAM

10 servings

Try this dish for your husband's birthday dinner! It will be a hit.

Preheat oven to 350°.

Debone, halve, and pound flat:

**5 chicken breasts**

On each flattened chicken breast cut to fit and place one of each:

**10 slices Country ham**

**10 slices Swiss cheese**

Roll up and secure each breast with two toothpicks. Place in an oblong baking dish. Cover with *Curry Sauce Cara.*

Top with:

**½ cup grated Cheddar cheese**
**¼ cup buttered bread crumbs**

Bake for one hour. Serve with *Sweet Potato-Apple Casserole.*

## CURRY SAUCE CARA

Combine in a mixing bowl:

**1 ten ounce can cream of mushroom soup**
**½ cup sour cream**
**¼ cup mayonnaise**
**1 teaspoon lemon juice**

**½ to 1 teaspoon curry powder**
**1 four ounce can mushrooms, drained**
**½ cup sauterne (optional)**

Pour over chicken and ham roll-ups as directed in *Curried Chicken and Ham.*

# CHICKEN-HAM CRESCENTS

6 servings

This is a favorite dish for guests. Serve with baked sweet potatoes and *Holiday Cranberry Mold*.

Preheat oven to 400°.

In a frying pan with a lid melt:

>    **2 tablespoons butter or margarine**

Slowly brown:

>    **6 chicken thighs**

Add to chicken:

>    **½ cup hot water**
>    **1 chicken bouillon cube**

Cover and simmer 30 minutes. Remove chicken from broth. Cool. Carefully remove bones. Measure broth. Add water to equal one cup. Mix:

>    **3 tablespoons flour**
>    **¼ teaspoon paprika**
>    **1 cup evaporated milk**
>    **1 four ounce can mushrooms, drained or 1 cup sliced fresh mushrooms browned in butter**
>    **¼ cup white wine**

Add slowly to 1 cup broth. Cook till thick. In a small bowl combine with 6 tablespoons of sauce:

>    **1 cup chopped cooked ham**

Fill the cavity of each thigh with ham and sauce mixture. Open and separate:

>    **1 eight ounce can refrigerator crescent rolls**

Wrap each thigh in a roll. Place on baking sheet. Bake till golden brown. Serve with remaining sauce.

# HAM ROLLS ROBERT

6 servings

Preheat oven to 325°. Beat until light:

>    **1 egg**

Add and let stand until thoroughly blended:

>    **½ cup milk**
>    **1 cup diced white bread**
>    **1 cup chopped cooked chicken**

>    **½ cup chopped almonds**
>    **dash nutmeg**

Prepare:

>    **6 slices cooked ham**

On each slice spoon 3 tablespoons of chicken mixture. Roll up carefully and place in a shallow, buttered baking dish. Spoon *Sauce Robert* over this and bake until brown.

# SAUCE ROBERT

Makes 1¼ cups

This makes a delicious, light, fluffy sauce that can be used on vegetables, fowl, fish, or meat.

Melt:

    ¼ **stick butter**

Add and cook till bubbly:

    ¼ **cup flour**

Add slowly and cook until smooth:

    **1 cup milk**

Boil for one minute, stirring constantly. Stir into sauce with an electric beater:

    ½ **pound Cheddar cheese, grated**

Add a little at a time:

    **4 ounces light beer**

Beat for at least 15 minutes.


# VIRGINIA HAM - VEAL FOLDOVERS

8 servings

This casserole and sauce can be prepared ahead of time and baked just before serving. Serve with *Sour Cream Rice Casserole,* asparagus spears, and *Tart Cherry Salad.*

Preheat oven to 350°.

Pound with a meat pounder until about 7½ by 4½ inches:

    **8 veal cutlets**

In the center of each cutlet, place one of:

    **8 thin slices Country ham**
    **8 thin slices Swiss cheese**

Fold veal over to cover ham and cheese. Secure with toothpicks. Brush outside of foldovers with:

    **2 ounces melted butter**

Then roll in:

    **1½ cups cornflake crumbs**

Place foldovers in ungreased oblong baking dish. Cover with foil. Bake in oven for 30 minutes. While casserole is baking, prepare sauce.

Combine:

    **1 ten ounce can golden cream of mushroom soup**
    ½ **cup milk**
    **2 tablespoons sauterne (optional)**

Spoon sauce over the cooked foldovers and bake 30 minutes longer, until tender.

# VEAL AND HAM PASTA

4 to 6 servings

This is a great company dish! It also lends itself well to freezing. Serve with a *French Bread* and a lettuce salad.

Cut into small pieces about ½ inch in size:

**1½ pounds veal steak**

Sprinkle with:

**salt and pepper**

Brown veal in:

**¼ stick butter or margarine**

Add:

**1 to 1½ cups sliced mushrooms**
**1 cup chopped green pepper**
**1 cup chopped onion**
**1 cup chopped cooked ham**

Saute for about 10 minutes, stirring frequently. Add:

**1 fifteen ounce can tomato sauce**

**1 sixteen ounce can stewed tomatoes, mashed**
**¼ cup tomato paste**
**1 teaspoon granulated garlic**
**½ teaspoon oregano**
**¼ teaspoon black pepper**

Simmer, covered, for about 45 minutes. Adjust seasonings to taste. Cook according to package directions:

**1 eight ounce package spaghetti**

Drain and stir into the cooked sauce until well blended. Serve at once. On each plate sprinkle:

**grated Parmesan cheese**

This also makes a marvelous casserole. Alternate layers of spaghetti and sauce with your favorite cheese, making sure cheese is the last layer. Bake 20 minutes at 350° until cheese melts. For variety, substitute spinach noodles or any other favorite pasta for spaghetti.

# HAM AND STEAK ROLL

8 servings

Dixie Peachy's excellent company dish can be made ahead.

Pound with a meat mallet:

**2 round steaks, cut ½ inch thick**

Brush one side of steak with:

**2 tablespoons melted butter**

Combine:

**2 cups ground cooked ham**
**½ cup coffee cream**
**1 tablespoon mustard**

Spread mixture on meat and roll up

like a jelly-roll. Tie with string. Sprinkle the two meat rolls with:

**4 tablespoons flour**
**⅛ teaspoon pepper**

Brown steak roll in a covered skillet in:

**2 tablespoons butter or shortening**

Add:

**1 sixteen ounce can tomatoes**

Cover and simmer 2 hours or until meat is tender. Slice like a jelly roll and serve on a platter with rice. Pour sauce over rice and sliced meat roll.

# HAM STUFFED TENDERLOIN TIP

4 to 6 servings

Mrs. Howard Gwaltney, Jr. of the Gwaltney Ham family, shared this favorite way of using leftover ham.

Preheat oven to 325°.

Slice open, without cutting all the way through, to resemble an open hotdog bun:

**1 whole tenderloin tip**

Split each half section again.

Combine to make stuffing:

**½ cup ground cooked ham**
**¾ cup finely chopped celery**
**¼ cup minced onion**
**1 slice bread, cubed**
**1 egg**
**½ teaspoon sage**
**1 four ounce can chopped mushrooms (optional)**

Sprinkle loin with:

**salt and pepper**

Stuff the split half-sections, then spoon stuffing in middle of tenderloin. Roll up jelly-roll fashion and tie or secure with toothpicks. Place in an oblong baking dish. Cover with foil. Bake for 45 minutes. Uncover and let brown for 15 more minutes.

# HAM AND SHRIMP JAMBALAYA

4 generous servings

This is a delightful dinner-party dish. *Sweet and Sour Salad* completes the meal.

Fry until crisp, remove from pan, and drain on paper towel:

**5 slices bacon**

Fry over medium heat in the bacon grease until tender:

**1 cup coarsely chopped green pepper**
**1 cup coarsely chopped onion**
**1 cup coarsely chopped celery**
**2 garlic cloves, minced**

Add:

**1½ cups chopped cooked ham**
**1 ten ounce can chicken broth**
**1 fifteen ounce can tomato sauce**
**¾ cup water**
**1 cup uncooked long grain rice**

Add the following seasonings:

**1 bay leaf**
**¼ teaspoon thyme**
**⅛ teaspoon cayenne**
**⅛ teaspoon black pepper**

Bring to a boil, cover and simmer 30 to 35 minutes, stirring occasionally until rice is tender. While this is cooking, bring to a boil:

**2 to 3 quarts water**

Add:

**1 to 1½ pounds raw shrimp**

Bring to boil again and cook 3 minutes. Drain, cool, and shell shrimp. Add shrimp to jambalaya mixture and serve, garnished with the crumbled bacon.

# GEORGIA GOVERNOR'S GUMBO

Mrs. George Busbee, wife of Georgia's governor, uses ham along with the other meats in her savory gumbo.

In a large soup kettle or Dutch oven, sauté until crisp:

**½ pound bacon**

Crumble bacon and reserve. In bacon drippings sauté:

**½ cup chopped scallions and tops
2 large onions, chopped
1 large clove garlic, minced
1 bell pepper, minced**

Add and brown to make a "roux":

**4 to 5 tablespoons plain flour**

Gradually add:

**5 cups water
2 teaspoons salt (omit if ham is salty)
1 teaspoon dried thyme
¼ teaspoon coarsely ground black pepper
2 one pound cans tomatoes and liquid**

**2 bay leaves
2 tablespoons chopped fresh parsley**

Cover pot and simmer slowly for 2 hours. Add:

**2 ten ounce packages frozen okra
2 cups diced cooked ham
1 teaspoon Creole seasoning (optional)
3 drops Tabasco**

Simmer 15 minutes, then add:

**2 pounds cooked shelled shrimp
1 pound crabmeat**

Simmer, uncovered, 10 minutes. Remove from heat. Just before serving add:

**1½ teaspoons gumbo filé powder (optional)**

Into serving bowls spoon:

**hot fluffy cooked rice**

Ladle gumbo over rice, sprinkle with bacon bits and serve.

# VIRGINIA HAM AND SWEETBREADS WITH MARSALA SAUCE

6 servings

Sweetbreads are a very delicately flavored variety meat, the pancreas glands from lamb, young steers and calves. When fresh they should be light, bright, and rosy in color.

Soak for 45 minutes in ice water to cover:

**3 pairs calf sweetbreads**

Drain and place sweetbreads in a skillet with enough water to cover. Add:

**1 teaspoon lemon juice or vinegar
1 teaspoon salt**

Bring to a boil, simmer 3 to 5 minutes. Cool sweetbreads in ice water and remove all connective tissue and covering. Split open the sweetbreads and sprinkle with:

**salt
pepper
¼ cup melted butter**

Place on broiler and broil about 5 minutes or until well browned. Include on the broiler at the same time:

**12 mushroom caps**

Layer on a platter:

**6 slices toast**
**6 slices cooked Country ham**

Top with the broiled mushrooms and sweetbreads, spoon on *Marsala Sauce* and serve at once.

---

## MARSALA SAUCE

---

In a skillet melt:

**2 tablespoons butter**

Add:

**2 tablespoons flour**

Stir until well blended. Add:

**1½ cups chicken stock**

Beat together:

**1 egg yolk**
**½ cup cream**

Pour into stock. Cook 2 minutes while stirring, then add:

**3 tablespoons Marsala or sherry**

Stir until well blended.

---

## PEANUT STUFFED HAM ROLLS SUFFOLK

---

8 to 10 servings

This is a great way of using up Christmas leftovers...a real gourmet's delight...good for a New Year's luncheon or for any dinner party.

Preheat oven to 325°.

Mix:

**1 cup cooked wild rice**
**½ cup salted peanuts**

Have ready:

**8 to 10 slices Virginia or Country ham**

In center of each slice place:

**3 tablespoons rice-peanut mixture**

Roll up ham slices and place in a shallow buttered baking dish, seam side down. Cover with *Mushroom Sauce.* Bake until brown and bubbly or about 25 minutes.

## MUSHROOM SAUCE

Saute:

**2 tablespoons butter**
**1 cup sliced fresh mushrooms or**
**1 four ounce can sliced**
**mushrooms, drained**

Add and stir in very well:

**2 tablespoons flour**

Gradually stir in:

**¾ cup chicken stock**
**½ cup half and half**

Cook until thickened and season with:

**2 tablespoons sherry**

## HAM ROLLED BROCCOLI

4 servings

Cook for just a few minutes:

**1 ten ounce package frozen**
**broccoli**

Drain and cool. Roll each broccoli spear in one of:

**8 slices Virginia or**
**Country ham**

Turn the bud ends of broccoli to outside and secure with toothpicks. Place rolls in a casserole dish and cover with *Sauce Robert.* Bake 15 minutes until bubbly and serve with herb rice and *Curried Pineapple Rings* for a complete meal.

## CRAB AND HAM MONET

6 servings

Sauté lightly:

**1 stick butter**
**1 small bunch green onions,**
**chopped**

Add:

**½ cup chopped parsley**
**2 tablespoons flour**

Add and blend:

**8 ounces half and half**
**½ pound Swiss cheese, grated**
**1 tablespoon sherry**
**1 cup minced cooked ham**

Fold in:

**1 pound lump crabmeat**

Serve in individual shell ramekins or:

**6 pastry shells, warmed**

# CRABMEAT AND VIRGINIA HAM MONROE

4 servings

This is an elegant way to serve ham. Use individual ramekins, preferably those shaped like shells. I serve this with baked potatoes and a tossed salad.

Pick over:

**1 pound crabmeat**

Sprinkle with:

**1 teaspoon lemon juice**

Sauté crabmeat in:

**1 stick butter**

Add:

**½ cup minced cooked Country ham**

Toss lightly and continue cooking until crabmeat is hot. Serve at once in warm ramekins. Garnish each serving with:

**1 sprig parsley**
**1 wedge lemon**

# CRAB-STUFFED HAM ROLLS WITH CURRY SAUCE CARA

6 servings

Preheat oven to 375°.

Pick over:

**1 pound crabmeat**

Divide crabmeat evenly among:

**12 thin slices cooked ham**

Roll up stuffed ham slices and place seam side down in a dish. Pour *Curry Sauce Cara* over ham rolls, cover, and bake for 20 minutes or until heated through.

# RUSH SPECIAL

8 to 10 servings

Mr. Churchill Young, owner of the Todd Ham Company, founded in 1779 and the oldest ham operation in the United States, reminisced, "One of my fondest memories as a youngster was going to the Commonwealth Club with my father and on one occasion he had some guests. The black head waiter was named Rush and was a real character...he would recite Lee's Farewell Address when encouraged to do so with 'a little paper.' The menu featured that day was *Rush Special* ...one of my favorite ways to eat Virginia Ham."

Mr. Franc Mayr, Manager of the Commonwealth Club, a very old established men's club in Richmond, Virginia, informed me that Rush's name was William Nathaniel James

Rush and that he had been there for fifty-three years. The recipe that follows was Rush's own creation for serving Virginia ham, and is still featured on the menu at this distinguished club. It is also a favorite of Virginia's lawmakers, according to State Senator J. Lewis Rawls, Jr.

Drain liquor from:

**1 quart oysters**

Place oysters in a heavy iron skillet with:

**1 tablespoon Worcestershire sauce (optional)**

**2 tablespoons melted butter**
**¼ teaspoon celery salt**

Sauté until oysters are done, turning often. Sprinkle with paprika. Drain and serve 3 or 4 oysters over each stack of 2 to 3 per serving:

**16 to 30** *Corn Cakes*

Top each stack with one of:

**8 to 10 slices broiled Virginia or Country ham**

Cover with a glass bell to keep oysters from drying out. Serve at once with the oyster liquor in a side bowl.

## CORN CAKES

Combine:

**2 cups water-ground corn meal**
**2 eggs**
**3 cups milk**
**4 tablespoons melted butter**
**½ teaspoon salt**
**1 tablespoon sugar**

**1 teaspoon baking powder**

Drop by spoonsful (enough batter to make a 4 inch diameter cake) onto a heated grill or skillet. Cook on one side, brown on the other. Place on a warmed plate; top with ham and oysters in *Rush Special.*

## STUFFED EGGPLANT

4 servings

Have a fresh eggplant on hand? Try this delicious dish—my mother-in-law gave it a triple star!

Preheat oven to 400°. Cut the top end off or cut in half lengthwise:

**1 medium or 2 small eggplants**

Scoop out pulp to within half an inch of outer skin. Sauté for 10 minutes with eggplant pulp:

4 tablespoons butter
½ cup chopped onion
1 cup chopped mushrooms

Add:

1 cup chopped cooked ham
¼ teaspoon salt
(omit if ham is salty)
⅛ teaspoon pepper

Fill eggplant shell with this mixture. Top with:

¼ cup buttered bread crumbs
grated Parmesan cheese

Bake until thoroughly heated through and brown, about 25 to 30 minutes. Serve by placing across top:

pimiento strips

It is also good topped with grated Swiss or Mozzarella cheese. The eggplant looks like a candle when the cheese melts and runs down the sides.

## HAM-STUFFED ZUCCHINI

8 servings

This is a delicious way of using bits of ham left over from Sunday's dinner. It is a complete meal when served with a salad.

Preheat oven to 375°.

Slice in half lengthwise then boil 5 to 7 minutes just enough to make tender:

8 medium zucchini or
yellow squash

Drain and scoop out pulp without breaking skin. Chop pulp and reserve. Brown in a skillet over medium heat and then drain on paper towel:

½ pound lean ground beef

Combine with browned hamburger and pulp from squash and mix well:

1 egg, slightly beaten
2 tablespoons grated Parmesan
or Romano cheese
¼ teaspoon pepper
½ teaspoon leaf basil
1 cup ground or finely chopped
cooked ham

Stuff zucchini shells with the mixture and place in a lightly greased baking dish just large enough to fit the squash. To make sauce, fry in a skillet and drain:

2 slices bacon

Add to bacon grease and fry until browned:

1 tablespoon chopped parsley
¼ cup chopped onion

Stir in and bring to a boil, then turn down and simmer 5 minutes:

8 ounces tomato juice
¾ cup water
crumbled bacon bits

Pour over zucchini. Top with:

½ cup grated Swiss cheese

Bake for 30 to 40 minutes. For variety, add ¼ cup chopped green pepper and ¼ cup chopped pimiento to stuffing mixture.

# LINCOLN HAM

2 servings

This recipe is known as Lincoln Ham, north of "You-Know-Where," according to Pearson Mapes, author and television producer of shows such as the Miss America Pageant.

Preheat oven to 400°.

Soak, covered with water, for 1 hour:

**1 inch thick Country ham steak**

Boil ham steak in fresh water for 15 minutes. Drain, place in baking dish and spread on both sides:

**Dijon type mustard**

Sprinkle top with:

**dark brown sugar**
**dash pepper**

Gently add just enough to cover ham steak:

**milk**

Bake 30 minutes. Remove to warm platter. Pour juices over steak and serve with *Baked Grits*, snap beans, and *Sweet Potatoes with Apples*.

# HONEY-GLAZED HAM STEAK CHERI

2 servings

Place in a shallow pan:

**1 ham steak about ½ inch thick**

Broil seven minutes on each side or until brown. Brush on ham steak a mixture of:

**4 tablespoons honey**
**1 tablespoon prepared mustard**

Place under broiler for about 10 minutes. If a Country ham steak is used, boil for about 10 minutes before broiling.

# HAM STEAK CECIL

1 serving

Cecil L. Webb, former executive chef at the United Virginia Bank/Seaboard National in Norfolk, Virginia often prepared this dish for the executives and their guests.

Layer in a baking dish:

**1 slice baked ham, ¼ to ½ inch thick**
**1 slice pineapple**
**2 slices Swiss cheese**

Bake in 450° oven until cheese is soft and slightly brown. Top with *Pineapple Raisin Sauce*.

# BARBECUED HAM STEAK

4 to 6 servings

Place in a large fry pan:

**2 uncooked sugar-cured ham steaks, 1 inch thick**

Cover with water. Parboil 5 minutes. Pour off water. Cover with marinade mixture:

**1 cup cider**
**3 tablespoons brown sugar**

**1 tablespoon dry mustard**
**3 whole cloves, crushed**

Let ham soak in marinade, off heat, for 15 minutes. Remove steaks, saving marinade, and slash fat. Grease grill with a piece of ham fat and place ham steaks on grill over medium hot coals. Baste with marinade, turning frequently, allowing 25 to 30 minutes total cooking time.

# HAM LOAF

8 servings

Mix in a large bowl:

**1½ pounds ground cooked sugar-cured ham**
**1½ pounds ground fresh pork**
**1 cup bread crumbs**
**1 scant cup milk**

Mold into a loaf and refrigerate overnight. Mix and use to coat loaf:

**¾ cup brown sugar**
**2 teaspoons dry mustard**

Bake in 350° oven for one hour. While cooking baste with:

**¼ cup pineapple juice**

While loaf cooks, cook quickly in a small amount of water, then drain:

**½ cup raisins**

Drain ham loaf and place on platter. Remove grease from drippings and add to drippings along with raisins and remaining juice from:

**1 thirteen ounce can pineapple chunks**

Dissolve and add to drippings:

**1½ tablespoons cornstarch**
**¼ cup water**

Cook over medium heat, stirring constantly until sauce thickens. Serve with *Ham Loaf.*

# KASSIE'S WEST VIRGINIA HAM LOAF

6 servings

Preheat oven to 350°. Grind together:

**1½ pounds cooked smoked ham**
**½ pound fresh pork**

Mix with the ground meats:

**1 cup bread crumbs**
**1 cup milk**

**1 egg**
**½ cup chopped celery**
**½ cup chopped onion**
**dash thyme**

Form into two loaves. Bake 15 to 20 minutes, then baste about three times with *Kassie's Sweet-Sour Sauce* while cooking another 35 to 40 minutes. This loaf may be frozen before or after it is cooked.

# KASSIE'S SWEET-SOUR SAUCE

Use this sauce for basting *Kassie's Ham Loaf* or for a ham steak. Mix:

**½ cup brown sugar**
**¼ cup vinegar**
**½ teaspoon dry mustard**

# GLAZED HAM RING WITH RED DEVIL SAUCE

8 to 10 servings

Minnielee Toler, artist from the Outer Banks, says that "this is one of the best meat loaves I have ever tasted, as the ham flavor is the strong one."

Preheat oven to 350°. Combine and mix well:

**about 1 pound ground cooked ham**
**1 pound ground beef**
**½ cup chopped onion**
**3 ounces milk**
**¾ cup fine cracker crumbs**

**1 egg, slightly beaten**
**½ ten ounce can tomato soup**

Pack lightly into a ring mold or form in a ring on an inch deep baking sheet or pack lightly into a 9½ x 5 x 3 inch loaf pan. Brush with *Red Devil Sauce* before and during baking. Bake for about 1 hour. Pour off excess fat. Let stand 5 minutes, then turn out on a platter. Fill the center of the ring with warm potato salad, whipped potatoes, or green peas with small potatoes. Serve with *Red Devil Sauce*.

# RED DEVIL SAUCE

Mix:

½ ten ounce can tomato soup
1 egg, slightly beaten
2 tablespoons prepared mustard
1 tablespoon vinegar

**1 tablespoon butter**
**1 tablespoon sugar**

Cook, stirring constantly, just until mixture thickens. Serve with *Glazed Ham Ring.*

# BAKED HAM SQUARES

6 servings

Preheat oven to 350°. Combine and mix well in a bowl:

**about 1½ cups ground smoked cooked ham**
**1 cup seasoned bread crumbs**
**2 eggs, slightly beaten**
**1 tablespoon minced onion**
**½ teaspoon dry mustard**
**1 cup milk**
**1 tablespoon chopped parsley**

**½ cup chopped celery**
**2 tablespoons butter**
**½ teaspoon salt (omit if ham is salty)**

Spoon into greased eight inch square pan or baking dish. Pat down and bake for 30 to 40 minutes; it gets crusty around the edges when done. Cut into squares and serve with *Creamy Corn Pudding,* garden peas, and *Jellied Pears.*

# CARAMEL UPSIDE DOWN SQUARES

Preheat oven to 350°. Combine in a mixing bowl:

**2 cups ground sugar-cured ham**
**¼ pound ground beef**
**2½ slices milk-soaked bread**
**½ cup milk**
**¼ teaspoon salt**
**2 beaten eggs**
**¼ teaspoon dry mustard**

On bottom of casserole dish distribute evenly:

**5 tablespoons brown sugar**
**6 pineapple slices**

Press meat on top of sugar and pineapple slices and bake for 1 hour. Slice; turn upside down and serve.

*Pineapple-Raisin Sauce* (omitting the ½ cup crushed pineapple and adding ½ cup more raisins) is delicious over the squares.

# HAM MOLDS

4 servings

Preheat oven to 350°. Combine:

**4 lightly beaten eggs**
**1¼ cups milk**
**½ teaspoon salt (omit if ham is salty)**
**1 teaspoon onion flakes**
**½ teaspoon pepper**
**dash paprika**
**1 cup ground or chopped cooked ham**

Pour into 4 buttered custard cups and set in a pan of water 1 inch deep. Bake until firm, about 25 minutes. Let cool; run knife around molds before turning out, if necessary. Unmold and serve with *White Sauce with Cheese*. You can add sliced mushrooms to the sauce, or use canned mushroom soup in lieu of white sauce.

# WHITE SAUCE WITH CHEESE

Makes 1 cup

This is the perfect sauce for *Ham Molds*.

In a saucepan melt:

**2 tablespoons butter**

Stir in:

**2 tablespoons flour**

Gradually add and stir constantly over medium heat until thickened:

**1 cup milk**

Stir in:

**½ cup grated Cheddar cheese**
**dash cayenne**

If sauce is a little too thick, add a little more milk and blend well.

## THE REAL "HAM" BURGER WITH SOUR CREAM SAUCE

Makes 8

Grind:

**4 cups cooked ham**

Combine with ground ham:

**1 cup soft bread crumbs**
**½ cup finely chopped onion**
**2 slightly beaten eggs**
   **dash pepper**

Shape mixture into 8 patties. Brown patties slowly on both sides in a small amount of hot fat. Remove patties from pan. To pan drippings add:

**1 cup sour cream**

Heat sour cream just until hot. Serve with patties. Garnish with:

**chopped chives or chopped green onion tops**

## HAM AND POTATO CROQUETTES

Makes 8

The proportions of ham and potatoes can be varied according to what is available in your kitchen. If you're in a hurry, use instant mashed potatoes, omitting the salt. The total mixture should yield about 3 cups.

Combine, then chill and shape in 8 croquettes:

**2 cups ground or minced cooked Country ham**
**1 cup mashed potatoes**
**1 tablespoon chopped onion**
**1 tablespoon chopped parsley**

**1 egg, slightly beaten (optional)**
   **dash pepper**

Combine:

**1 tablespoon water**
**1 beaten egg**

Dip croquettes into egg mixture and roll in:

**fine dry bread crumbs or cracker crumbs**

Brown croquettes in small amount of oil or bacon drippings. You can also deep fry these.

# OLD-FASHIONED HAM CROQUETTES

Makes 8

For a traditional favorite way to serve ham, try these. Serve with your favorite potato dish and buttered broccoli.

Make ½ cup thick white sauce; melt over low heat:

**2 tablespoons butter**

Stir in:

**2 tablespoons flour**

Stir until flour is well-blended. Slowly stir in:

**½ cup milk**

Stir until sauce is thick. Cool and mix with:

**2 cups ground cooked Country ham**

Shape into croquettes. Beat together:

**1 egg**
**2 tablespoons water**

Dip each croquette into egg mixture, then into:

**½ cup cracker meal**

Let sit about 30 minutes. In a deep fat fryer heat to 365°:

**3 inches oil**

Put croquettes in fryer basket, lower into hot oil until golden brown. Drain on paper towels. Garnish with:

**chopped parsley**

# BAKED HAM CROQUETTES

8 servings

Preheat oven to 350°. Mix:

**2½ cups ground cooked ham**
**1 egg, slightly beaten**

Add just enough to cause the mixture to hold together:

**¼ cup (approx.) milk**
**¼ to ½ cup (approx.) unsalted cracker crumbs**

Shape the mixture into 8 round flat patties and roll in crumbs. Dip each patty into:

**1 egg, slightly beaten**

Roll once again in cracker crumbs. Sprinkle on top of each patty:

**paprika**

Place on a greased cookie sheet. Bake 30 to 40 minutes until brown. Garnish with:

**parsley**

I make my own crumbs by putting crackers between sheets of wax paper and rolling until fine. When the patties are shaped and dipped, put them on layers of wax paper on a plate, refrigerate until they firm up nicely, then bake.

# SURPRISE CROQUETTES

Makes 10

Mash in the saucepan in which they were cooked:

**2 cups cooked chopped potatoes, drained**

Add:

**4 tablespoons cream or milk**
**1 teaspoon onion juice**
**dash salt**
**dash pepper**

Stir over low heat until hot and smooth. Remove from heat, cool slightly. Stir in:

**2 egg yolks, beaten**

Form into 10 cylinders or cone shapes.

Make a depression in each and into each hole, put one of:

**10 tablespoons minced cooked ham**

Press the potato around the filling. Roll croquettes in:

**flour**

Beat together slightly, then dip croquettes in mixture of:

**2 egg whites**
**1 tablespoon water**

Roll croquettes in:

**½ cup plain or seasoned bread crumbs**

Fry in deep fat until golden brown.


# LUAU HAMBALLS

8 servings

Preheat oven to 350°. Combine:

**1 pound ground cooked ham**
**½ pound ground fresh pork**
**¾ cup soft bread crumbs**
**2 eggs, slightly beaten**
**½ cup milk**

**¼ cup onion flakes or minced onion**

Shape into 8 balls and place hamballs in baking pan or casserole dish. Mix *Luau Sauce* and spoon over hamballs. Bake for 1 hour. Serve with *Sour Cream Rice Casserole* and a fresh green vegetable.


# LUAU SAUCE

Combine:

**1 nine ounce can crushed pineapple**
**5 tablespoons ketchup**

**5 tablespoons vinegar**
**2 tablespoons soy sauce**
**1½ teaspoons powdered ginger**
**½ cup brown sugar**
**dash pepper**

# SWEET AND SOUR SAUCE HAMBALLS

6 to 8 servings

Preheat oven to 350°. Combine:

**1 pound ground cooked ham**
**½ pound ground fresh pork**
**1 cup fine dry bread crumbs**
**1 cup evaporated milk**
**2 eggs**

Shape into 6 to 8 balls and place in baking dish or casserole dish. Mix

sweet and sour sauce:

**1 cup brown sugar**
**¼ cup vinegar**
**½ cup water**
**½ teaspoon dry mustard**

Pour sauce over balls and bake for 1 hour. Baste every 30 minutes. A congealed fruit salad and sweet potatoes go well with this. For cocktails, make walnut-sized balls.

# SWEET AND SOUR CABBAGE ROLLS

4 servings

Preheat oven to 350°. Immerse in boiling water for about 3 minutes until limp, then drain:

**4 large cabbage leaves**

Soak in hot water for 15 minutes then drain:

**½ cup raisins**

Combine with raisins:

**½ cup cooked rice**
**¼ cup finely minced onion**

**1 cup ground cooked ham**
**1 egg, beaten**

Spoon about 2 tablespoons of mixture on each cabbage leaf. Roll up sandwich-wrap fashion and place in casserole dish, seam side down. Make sauce by mixing:

**3 tablespoons cold water**
**½ cup brown sugar**
**5 tablespoons lemon juice**
**½ cup seedless raisins**

Pour over cabbage rolls. Bake 1½ hours.

# GLAZES

Hams are usually decorated in the traditional manner of scoring (making diagonal slashes in the fat with a sharp knife to form diamond shapes, studding with whole cloves and glazing. A distinctive flavor can be achieved with a glaze, and this is done the last 30 minutes of baking the ham. Cooking instructions are found on pages 31 to 35.

In the 1824 cookbook *The Virginia Housewife* written by Mary Randolph, a relative of Thomas Jefferson, the process was described as toasting a ham instead of glazing: "To toast a ham, boil it well, take off the skin, and cover the top thickly with bread crumbs, put it in an oven to brown and serve it up."

## GLAZES FOR COUNTRY OR VIRGINIA HAM

Glazes for country and Virginia hams are traditionally kept simple. After the ham has been fully cooked, remove the skin and trim off the excess fat. Score the fat, then use one of the following glazes.

## GRANDMOTHER HARRELL'S GLAZE

Sprinkle the ham with white sugar, stud the diamond shapes scored in the fat with whole cloves. Bake in a 300° oven for about 30 minutes or until nicely browned.

## BROWN SUGAR GLAZE I

Rub cooked ham with:

**1 cup brown sugar**

Sprinkle over the top:

**½ cup bread crumbs**

Bake at 300° for 30 minutes.

## BROWN SUGAR GLAZE II

Combine:

**4 tablespoons prepared mustard**
**1 cup brown sugar**

Spread evenly over ham. Bake about 10 to 15 minutes in a 375° oven.

## HONEY-MUSTARD GLAZE

This is recommended for Country, Virginia and smoked hams. Combine:

**2 tablespoons prepared mustard**
**1 cup brown sugar**
**½ cup honey**

Spread mixture over cooked ham. Garnish with:

**pineapple rings**

In the center of each ring secure with toothpicks:

**maraschino cherries**

Bake at 300° for 30 minutes.

## GRANDMAMA JONES' WINE AND HONEY GLAZE

Martha Jones, my husband's grandmother, prefers this glaze for her baked hams. It also gives the house a delightful aroma.

Cook ham by the "Kettle Method." Remove skin, score the fat and stud with:

**cloves**

Coat ham with:

**½ cup (approx.) honey**

Baste with:

**white port wine**

Bake about 30 minutes in a 300° oven. Baste every 10 minutes with pan juices and additional wine.

# SWEET CIDER GLAZE

Mix:

**1 cup brown sugar**
**½ cup apple cider**

Baste cooked ham with this glaze; brown in a 375° oven for about thirty minutes.

# CHAMPAGNE HAM

This was a nineteenth century innovation first described in *Key to the Pantry* in 1898. It is delicious. Virginia Gearhart Gray, historian and lecturer on cookbooks, marked this recipe as of special interest and significance in her family collection. Her daughter, Miss Sally Gray, cookbook author and librarian at the College of William and Mary, shared this with me.

Rub a whole cooked ham with:

**brown sugar**

Combine:

**1 tablespoon allspice**
**1 teaspoon ground cloves**
**1 cup vinegar**
**1 cup Champagne**
**½ cup sugar**

Pour over top of ham and bake slowly, 300°, for 1 hour. Add:

**1 cup Champagne**

Serve pan juices as gravy for ham.

# GLAZES FOR SMOKED,
## SUGAR-CURED OR TENDERIZED HAMS

The word smoked ham appears on the majority of packers' labels, however the terms smoked, sugar-cured and tenderized are synonomous. This type of ham lends itself well to fruit glazes. Use your imagination and combine fresh fruits or canned fruits. Marmalades and preserves also make a glaze that will enhance the smoked flavor of this milder ham.

## JELLY GLAZE

Combine and beat until smooth:

- ¼ **cup ham juices (pan drippings or ham stock)**
- 1 **cup currant jelly, orange marmalade, cranberry jelly, apricot preserves or pineapple preserves**

1 **teaspoon dry mustard**
**dash cinnamon**
**dash ground cloves**

Spread on ham last 30 minutes of baking.

## ORANGE GLAZE

Combine:

- 1 **cup brown sugar**
- 1 **tablespoon cornstarch**
- 1 **teaspoon prepared mustard**
- 1 **six ounce can frozen concentrated orange juice**

½ **teaspoon ground ginger**

Spread over ham about 20 to 30 minutes before ham is done. Return ham to oven to finish cooking and set the glaze. This glaze is especially delicious with a smoked ham.

## PINEAPPLE-CHERRY GLAZED CANNED HAM

Sugar-cured hams lend themselves to a delicious fruit glaze.

Preheat oven to 325°. Heat for 1½ hours:

**1 five pound canned ham**

Meanwhile, combine in a saucepan:

**juice from 1 pound can sliced pineapple**
**¾ cup cherry preserves**

**⅛ teaspoon cinnamon**
**dash allspice**

Cook until mixture thickens and is reduced by about half. Arrange on top of ham:

**pineapple slices from 1 pound can**

Spoon cherry sauce over ham and pineapple slices. Bake for 30 minutes longer.

## SPICY GLAZED HAM AND PEARS

Prepare canned ham, smoked ham, or ham steaks according to directions. The last 30 minutes of baking spread with the following glaze. Drain, reserving juice:

**1 pound can pears**

Combine:

**½ cup orange marmalade**

**4 tablespoons brown sugar**
**⅛ teaspoon allspice**
**⅛ teaspoon ground cloves**
**1 tablespoon prepared mustard**
**1 tablespoon pear juice**

Garnish the ham with pear halves and mint leaves and fill each pear cavity with a teaspoonful of the glaze.

# SAUCES

## FRUITED SAUCE WITH SMOKED HAM

Drain, reserving juice:

**1 pound can fruit cocktail**

Combine:

**juice from fruit cocktail**
**1 tablespoon cornstarch**
**¼ cup maraschino cherry juice**
**¼ cup pineapple juice**
**1 teaspoon lemon juice**

Cook until thickened. Spoon over a fully cooked 5 pound canned smoked ham. On top of sauce, place drained fruit cocktail. Garnish with:

**¼ cup pecan halves**

Garnish serving platter with fresh mint leaves if available.

## SPICY PLUM SAUCE

You can spoon some of this sauce over a fully cooked whole smoked ham, or a baked boneless ham before serving, or just serve over the top of ham slices on plates.

Drain and reserve syrup from:

**1 two pound can purple plums**

Cut plums in half and remove pits. Combine and add to plum syrup in a saucepan:

**3 tablespoons cornstarch**

**¼ teaspoon cinnamon**
**⅛ teaspoon allspice**
**dash salt**
**3 tablespoons sugar**

Cook over low heat, stirring constantly until thickened and clear. Add plum halves and:

**2 tablespoons lemon juice**
**1 tablespoon butter or margarine**

Cook until heated through.

# PECAN RAISIN SAUCE

Makes 2 cups

Combine:

- ½ cup brown sugar
- 1 teaspoon dry mustard
- 2 tablespoons cornstarch

- 2 tablespoons lemon juice
- ¼ teaspoon orange peel
- 1½ cups water
- ½ cup raisins
- ½ cup pecans

Stir over low heat until thick.

# PINEAPPLE-RAISIN SAUCE

Serve this sauce with ham steak or sliced ham. Combine in saucepan and bring to a boil over medium heat:

- 1 cup water
- ½ cup pineapple juice
- ½ cup raisins
- ½ cup crushed pineapple
- 1 slice lemon

- ½ cup sugar

Reduce heat, simmer for 3 minutes, then add to the sauce a well blended mixture of:

- 1 tablespoon cornstarch
- ¼ cup water

Cook until sauce thickens, then serve.

# RAISIN-CIDER SAUCE

Betty Blanton, First Lady of Tennessee, sent me her favorite sauce for ham.

In a saucepan, mix:

- ¼ cup brown sugar, firmly packed
- 1½ tablespoons cornstarch

Add:

- ⅛ teaspoon salt
- 1 cup apple cider
- 8 whole cloves
    dash cinnamon
- 1 tablespoon butter

Cook for 10 minutes, stirring constantly, until raisins are plump. Serve hot over baked ham slices.

# MARTHA CHERRY BARBECUE SAUCE FOR FRESH HAM

Fresh ham is really considered a roast of pork since it is the hind leg that has not been cured or smoked. This, however, makes a delicious entree. Serve with cole slaw and *Glazed Sweet Potatoes*.

Preheat oven to 350°. Place in an uncovered roasting pan and brown in the oven:

**1 uncured fresh 10 pound ham**

Turn ham frequently to brown all sides. Meanwhile, saute:

**1 medium onion, finely chopped**
**1 tablespoon butter**

Remove from heat and add:

**¾ cup ketchup**

¾ **cup water**
2 **tablespoons lemon juice**
1 **teaspoon salt**
¼ **teaspoon pepper**
2 **tablespoons brown sugar**
½ **teaspoon dry mustard**
1 **teaspoon paprika**
2 **tablespoons Worcestershire sauce**
½ **cup pineapple or orange juice or 1 teaspoon chili powder**

Stir well, return to heat, bring to boil. Cover and simmer for 10 minutes. Baste ham frequently for about three hours or until it is very tender. During the last half hour, pour remaining sauce over the ham. If sauce gets too thick, thin with a little water.

# KENTUCKY COUNTRY HAM WITH BOURBON SAUCE FLAMBE

1 serving

Charlann Carroll, wife of Julian Carroll, Governor of Kentucky, sent this favorite ham recipe of the First Family.

Brown in a heavy skillet:

**1 Country ham steak**

Pour off ham drippings leaving about 2 tablespoons in the pan. Mix in a small bowl:

**1 tablespoon light brown sugar**
**1 jigger bourbon**

Stir until sugar is dissolved, then add mixture to ham steak and flame. Voila!

## TOMATO ASPIC LOAF

6 to 8 servings

Soften in cold water:

**2 envelopes unflavored gelatin**

Bring to a boil:

**4 cups tomato juice**

Add gelatin and stir until dissolved. Add:

**1 teaspoon salt**
**2 tablespoons vinegar**
**2 tablespoons onion juice**
**1 bay leaf**
**1 teaspoon sugar**
**1 tablespoon chopped parsley**
**½ teaspoon ground cloves**
**dash pepper**
**1 teaspoon Worcestershire sauce**

Simmer for 5 minutes. Pour into a loaf mold. Cool until mixture begins to thicken, then add:

**½ cup chopped celery**
**½ cup chopped green pepper**
**½ cup finely diced cucumber**

Mix well then place in center of mold in middle of gelatin, making sure they are covered by gelatin:

**½ six-ounce can white asparagus spears**

Chill mold until firm. Unmold and decorate with:

**1 hard-cooked egg, sliced**
**mayonnaise**

## "PLAINS SPECIAL" CHEESE RING

A delightful accompaniment to a ham dinner, contributed by First Lady Rosalynn Carter.

Combine, seasoning to taste with pepper:

**1 pound grated sharp cheese**
**1 cup finely chopped nuts**
**1 cup mayonnaise**
**1 small onion, finely grated**

**black pepper**
**dash cayenne**

Mix well and place in a 5 or 6 cup lightly greased ring mold. Refrigerate until firm for several hours or overnight. To serve, unmold. If desired, fill center with:

**strawberry preserves (optional)**

Or serve plain with crackers.

# SWEET AND SOUR SALAD

4 servings

Combine in a salad bowl:

  1 small head lettuce, chopped
  1 medium Bermuda onion,
    thinly sliced
  2 whole oranges, segmented

Combine and toss with salad:

  1 cup sugar
  1 tablespoon corn oil
  1 cup vinegar
  1 teaspoon ginger
  dash salt
  dash lemon pepper

# APPLE-BERRY SALAD

8 servings

Stir until dissolved:

  1 three ounce package raspberry
    gelatin
  1 cup boiling water

Add:

  1 ten ounce package frozen
    raspberries

  1 cup applesauce
  1 cup sour cream
  1 cup miniature marshmallows

Pour into a mold or square pan and refrigerate. An alternative method is to congeal all of the ingredients except sour cream and marshmallows. Mix these and spread on top before cutting into squares and serving.

# APRICOT-BANANA MOLD MATTHEW

6 servings

Pour into a two cup measure:

  1 twelve ounce can apricot
    nectar

Drain juice from:

  1 four ounce can crushed
    pineapple

Pour enough pineapple juice in the nectar to equal two cups. Pour into a saucepan and bring to a boil. Pour over:

  1 three ounce package orange
    or apricot gelatin

Stir until dissolved. Cool and add along with drained pineapple:

2 or 3 mashed bananas
dash lemon juice
½ to ¾ cup chopped walnuts or
pecans

Pour into a mold and refrigerate until ready to serve. For an alternate way of serving, spread *Cooked Dressing* combined with whipped cream over the top of the unmolded salad. Sprinkle with grated cheese or coconut.

## HOLIDAY CRANBERRY MOLD

8 servings

Dissolve:

  2 three ounce packages lemon
  gelatin
  1¾ cup boiling water

Add:

  juice from 1 orange
  juice from 1 lemon

Cool until slightly thickened. Put through food chopper, grinder, or blender:

  1 pound cranberries
  rind from 1 orange

Add to cranberries:

  1 cup sugar
  1½ cups finely chopped celery
  1 cup chopped pecans

Combine cranberry mixture with slightly thickened gelatin mixture and pour into mold to chill. This is good served with *Cooked Dressing*.

## CRANBERRY SALAD WITH SOUR CREAM

6 servings

Stir until gelatin is dissolved:

  1 three ounce package cherry
  gelatin
  1½ cups boiling water

Refrigerate. When gelatin begins to thicken, stir in:

  1 pound can whole cranberry
  sauce

  ¼ cup chopped celery
  ½ cup chopped walnuts

Pour half of the mixture into a mold, spread evenly over the gelatin:

  1 cup sour cream

Top with remainder of mixture and chill until firm.

# TART CHERRY DELIGHT

6 servings

Combine in saucepan and bring to a boil:

> 1 pound can red tart sour cherries
> ¾ cup sugar

Add in separate bowl:

> 1 three ounce package cream cheese, softened

> 1 three ounce package cherry gelatin

Mix well. Pour hot cherry mixture over gelatin mix and stir until completely dissolved; cool. To this mixture add:

> 1 four ounce can crushed pineapple, drained
> ½ cup chopped pecans
> ½ cup cold water

Chill until firm.

# SHERRIED JELLY WITH PECAN BALLS

6 servings

Drain, reserving juice:

> 1 pound jar pitted Bing cherries
> 1 thirteen ounce can crushed pineapple

Dissolve:

> 1 three ounce package cherry gelatin
> 1 cup boiling water

Stir until well-blended, then add drained cherries and:

> ½ cup sherry
> ½ cup cherry juice

> 1 cup crushed pineapple

Pour into individual molds or dishes and chill until congealed. Combine in a small bowl and spread over the top of the salad or form in 1 inch balls and use to top molds:

> 1 eight ounce package cream cheese, softened
> ½ cup chopped pecans
> 2 teaspoons lemon juice
> 2 tablespoons sugar

Double the ingredients if you wish to use a ring mold.

# SUMMER CUCUMBER MOLD

8 servings

Dissolve in mixing bowl:

> 1 six ounce package lime gelatin
> 1 cup boiling water

Add:

> 2 large cucumbers, grated
> 1 medium onion, finely grated
> 1 cup sour cream

2 teaspoons vinegar
¼ teaspoon salt
½ cup mayonnaise

Blend well and pour in mold. Refrigerate until ready to use.

---

## LEMON VEGETABLE MOLD

---

8 servings

Dissolve:

**2 three ounce packages
lemon gelatin**
**1¾ cups boiling water**

Cool until slightly thickened. Stir in:

**1 cup shredded carrot**
**1 cup finely shredded red or
green cabbage**

**1 teaspoon celery seed**
**¼ cup chopped pimiento
(optional)**
**1 teaspoon sugar**
**1 teaspoon vinegar**
**1 diced cucumber (optional)**

Pour into mold and chill. Add a few radish roses before mixture is completely set. Serve with *Cooked Dressing*, using mayonnaise instead of whipped cream.

---

## LIME PARTY MOLD

---

8 servings

Dissolve:

**1 three ounce package
lime gelatin**
**¾ cup boiling water**

Add and stir well:

**¾ cup fruit juice from
drained fruit**

Stir into cooled gelatin mixture:

**1 eight ounce can crushed
pineapple, drained**
**1 eight ounce can pears, drained
and diced**
**1 eight ounce can white grapes,
drained**
**1 teaspoon lemon juice**
**8 ounces sour cream**

Pour into favorite mold and refrigerate.

# INDIVIDUAL SPICED PEACH MOLDS

8 servings

Excellent garnish for a platter of sliced ham.

In a large bowl soften and set aside:

**1 three ounce package orange or peach gelatin**
**1 envelope plain gelatin**
**½ cup cold water**

Drain into a 2 cup measure:

**syrup from 1 pound can sliced peaches**

Add enough to make 2 cups of liquid:

**orange juice**

Pour into a saucepan with:

**1 cup pickled peach syrup**

Bring to a boil and pour over gelatin mixture. Stir well and pour into 8 individual fluted four ounce molds enough gelatin mixture to cover bottom. Refrigerate until thickened slightly. Combine in a small bowl:

**1 eight ounce package cream cheese, softened**
**4 teaspoons finely minced crystallized ginger**

Shape into 8 balls and place one in each mold. Stand one slice of peach in each flute. Pour rest of gelatin mixture carefully around peach slices, covering outside; add extra peaches on top, if there is room. Chill again until firm. Serve on lettuce. If you wish to make only 4 individual molds, prepare the same amount of gelatin and save half for another time as it keeps well in the refrigerator. Simply melt and continue with the recipe.

# JELLIED PEARS

4 to 6 servings

This is nice with *Baked Ham Squares*. Drain and reserve syrup from:

**1 pound can pears**

Cut pears into ½ inch pieces. Soften:

**1 package unflavored gelatin**
**2 tablespoons pear syrup**

In a saucepan boil:

**½ cup pear syrup**

Remove from heat, pour syrup over:

**1 eight ounce package peach or apricot gelatin**

Stir until dissolved and add:

**1 twelve ounce can apricot nectar**
**1½ tablespoons lemon juice**

Stir together with chopped pears and gelatins:

**dash salt**
**1 four ounce can Mandarin oranges, drained**
**1 eight ounce can pineapple tidbits, drained**

Pour into a mold or dish. Refrigerate until firm. To double the recipe, double everything except the unflavored gelatin.

# CURRIED PINEAPPLE SALAD

8 servings

In large mixing bowl combine:

**2 three ounce packages lemon gelatin**

**1 teaspoon curry powder**

Add and stir until dissolved:

**2 cups boiling water**

Drain juice into a 16 ounce measuring cup from:

**1 eight ounce can crushed pineapple**

Add to the cup to make 16 ounces of liquid:

**2 tablespoons lemon juice cold water**

Stir into gelatin mixture. Pour a thin layer into an 8 inch square dish and chill until firm. Slice lengthwise into thirds and place on firm gelatin:

**1 banana**

Pour another layer of gelatin over banana. Chill until firm. Combine with remaining gelatin mixture and reserved crushed pineapple:

**2 sliced bananas**

**1 cup thinly sliced celery**

Pour over congealed mixture and chill until firm. Serve with *Cooked Dressing*.

# LAURA'S FRUIT SALAD

8 servings

This is tasty served with *Ham a la King*.

Stir until dissolved:

**1 three ounce package lemon gelatin**

**1 three ounce package orange gelatin**

**2 cups boiling water**

Stir in:

**1½ cups chilled orange juice**

When mixture is cool, add and pour into mold:

**1 pound can fruit cocktail, drained**

**1 can applesauce**

**2 cups chopped, peeled apple**

**½ cup chopped pecans**

**¼ cup chopped dates**

**¼ cup dark raisins**

**1 eight ounce can crushed pineapple, drained**

Refrigerate until set. Serve with *Cooked Dressing*.

# COOKED DRESSING

Makes 1½ cups

This dressing is delicious with fruit salads or congealed salads. It will keep in the refrigerator for several days.

Beat:

**2 eggs**

Add and beat well:

**3 tablespoons flour**
**½ cup sugar**

Add:

**1 cup pineapple juice**

Cook until thick, stirring constantly. Chill and just before serving stir in:

**½ cup mayonnaise or**
**whipped cream or**
**whipped topping**

Use to top congealed or fruit salads; sprinkle with:

**grated coconut or**
**grated cheese**

# FROZEN FRUIT SALAD

8 to 10 servings

This is especially nice with *Luncheon Quiche.* Mix:

**2 cups sour cream**
**2 tablespoons lemon juice**
**½ cup sugar**
**⅛ teaspoon salt**
**1 eight ounce can crushed**
**pineapple, drained**

**2 bananas, diced**
**1 sixteen ounce can Bing cherries,**
**pitted and drained**
**¼ cup chopped pecans**

Pour into a 9 by 13 inch dish and freeze. Remove from freezer 10 minutes before serving. Cut into squares.

# PINK CRANBERRY FREEZE

8 servings

This is a nice luncheon salad. Soften:

**2 three ounce packages**
**cream cheese**

Blend in:

**1 tablespoon mayonnaise**
**1 tablespoon lemon juice**

Add:

**3 tablespoons sugar**
**1 pound can whole cranberry**
**sauce**
**1 eight ounce can crushed**
**pineapple**
**½ cup chopped nuts**

Whip:

**1 cup whipping cream**

Add:

**½ cup powdered sugar**

**1 teaspoon vanilla**

Fold whipping cream mixture into cranberry mixture. Pour in a loaf pan. Freeze at least six hours. Cut into slices and serve on lettuce.

## GINGERED FRUIT

8 to 10 servings

This goes nicely with baked ham.

Preheat oven to 325°. Arrange in baking dish:

**1 pound can pear halves, with juice**

**1 pound can apricot halves, drained**

**1 eight ounce can pineapple chunks, drained**

**4 tablespoons chopped crystallized ginger**

**4 thin slices lemon, quartered**

**½ cup brown sugar**

**¼ cup maraschino cherries**

Bake uncovered for about 45 minutes. Serve hot or cold.

## STUFFED RED APPLES

6 to 9 servings ·

These make a beautiful accompaniment salad. They are festive as well as delicious—a little something different.

Core and as you peel, drop in cold water to prevent discoloring:

**6 to 9 whole cooking apples**

In a heavy skillet or saucepan place enough to cover apples half way so that when they are turned they will become red all over:

**2½ cups (approx.) cold water**
**1½ to 2 cups sugar**
**1 teaspoon (approx.) red food coloring**

Stir liquid and mix well; water should be very red. Add apples carefully, setting them up without crowding. Cook on medium low heat; just simmer

until tender when pricked; do not overcook or they will fall apart. Turn several times while cooking so apples will be a uniform color. Remove apples from the liquid and chill up to 2 hours before stuffing. The liquid that is left can be refrigerated and used again. For the stuffing mix well:

**1 eight ounce package cream cheese, softened**
**1 teaspoon mayonnaise**
**¼ cup chopped pecans**
**¼ cup raisins**

Add to stuffing mixture enough to make a stiff consistency:

**1 ounce (approx.) pineapple juice**

Spoon some of stuffing into each chilled apple. Serve on lettuce. For variation, drop a few cinnamon candies in the sugar water to give a spicy flavor.

# ABSOLUTELY PERFECT APPLESAUCE

6 to 8 servings

Preheat oven to 350°. Strain juice from:

**1 lemon**

Pour juice into a heavy ovenproof casserole. Peel, core and quarter:

**6 tart cooking apples**

Drop into pan, turn in juice so well-coated. Stir once again after all apples have been added. Cut to the shape of the top of the pan:

**brown paper bag or wax paper**

Butter one side generously and place buttered side down on top of apples; cover with lid to pan. Bake 45 minutes. When apples are cooked, stir in to taste:

**½ cup (approx.) sugar**

# FRIED APPLE RINGS

4 servings

Core but do not peel:

**3 large firm tart cooking apples**

Cut apples crosswise into quarter inch rings. Combine:

**½ cup sugar**
**1 teaspoon ground cinnamon**

Fry rings for 2 minutes on one side in:

**4 tablespoons melted margarine or butter**

Sprinkle with sugar mixture and turn to other side. Sprinkle with sugar mixture. Drain on paper towels. Place around platter of sliced ham.

# CURRIED PINEAPPLE RINGS

4 servings

Place in an oblong baking dish:

**4 pineapple slices**
**¼ cup pineapple juice**

Sprinkle each slice with:

**brown sugar**
**dash curry powder**

**dots of butter**

Broil until sugar and butter melt and rings are well glazed. Garnish a platter of ham with these rings, cherries, and parsley. For variety, add drained pears, peaches, and/or maraschino cherries to the pineapple in the baking dish, then continue with the glazing.

# FRIED PINEAPPLE

4 servings

Drain:

**1 eight ounce can sliced pineapple**

Dip each slice into:

¼ **cup flour**

Fry slices on medium heat until brown in:

**3 tablespoons corn oil**

Drain on paper towel and serve.

# BRANDIED PEACHES

Makes 3 pints

Dip into boiling water and peel:

**12 to 13 small perfect peaches**

In a pan boil for 10 minutes:

**6 cups water**
**4 cups sugar**

Cook peaches in the syrup a few at a time, until tender when tested with a toothpick, about 5 minutes. Pack into jars. Add to each pint:

**2 tablespoons brandy**

Fill the jars with syrup. Store one month before using.

# PICKLED PEACHES

Makes about 4 quarts

Wash and peel, leaving whole:

**24 or about 3½ pounds medium sized peaches**

In a large kettle, boil together about 10 minutes:

**3 cups sugar**

**1 cup vinegar**
**3 teaspoons whole cloves**

Drop a few peaches at a time into the boiling syrup and cook until peaches can be easily pierced with a fork, but remain a little firm. As they become tender, remove peaches one at a time and pack into hot sterilized jars. Cover with syrup and seal.

# AUNT MARGARET'S WATERMELON RIND PICKLE

Makes 2 pints

Peel and cut into cubes, leaving pink tinge on top:

**3 pounds watermelon rind**

Let stand overnight in a solution of:

**2 tablespoons salt**
**1 quart water**

Make enough solution to cover pickles. The next morning drain, cover rind with cold water, and cook until tender. Drain. In a separate saucepan combine:

**5 cups sugar**
**2 cups cider vinegar**

**1 cup cold water**

Tie the following in a spice bag made of a small piece of cheese cloth or muslin:

**1 tablespoon whole cloves**
**1 tablespoon whole allspice**
**1 tablespoon broken cinnamon stick**
**1 lemon, sliced**

Drop spice bag into syrup mixture. Boil for 5 minutes. Add watermelon rind and cook about 45 minutes or until transparent looking. Pack hot sterilized jars, 2 pints or 1 quart, with rind, cover with syrup and seal.

# HOMEMADE SWEET CUCUMBER PICKLE

Makes about 4 quarts

Wash thoroughly, scrubbing with a vegetable brush, medium sized cucumbers. Slice ¼ inch thick and weigh:

**7 pounds sliced cucumbers**

In a crock or large enameled pot, make a strong lime water soaking solution by mixing:

**3 cups lime**
**1 gallon water**

Add sliced cucumbers to lime solution and soak immersed for 24 hours. The next day, pour off the lime water. Place cucumbers in another pan. Rinse all the lime water out of the soaking container. Put cucumbers back in container and cover with fresh water. Let soak 2 hours. Change water again and continue this process 3 more times. Drain cucumbers. Make a syrup solution by combining:

**5 pounds sugar**
**3 pints vinegar**
**3 tablespoons pickling spice**

Bring to boil and place pickles in syrup. Cook for 1 hour after they start boiling. Pack in sterilized jars, cover with syrup, and seal jars. You may leave pickles in syrup overnight and cook the next day if it is more convenient. If any syrup is left, refrigerate and use again.

# BAKED BEANS

4 to 6 servings

*Baked Beans, Old-Fashioned Potato Salad* and sliced ham make a super picnic.

Preheat oven to 325°. Fry until crisp:

**4 slices bacon**

Sauté in bacon drippings:

**1 medium onion, chopped**
**1 four ounce can chopped mushrooms, drained**

Add:

**½ cup ketchup**

**2 tablespoons prepared mustard**
**¼ cup brown sugar**
**1 sixteen ounce can pork and beans**

Cook for 5 minutes. Pour into casserole dish. Bake for 45 minutes. Top with the crumbled bacon. Onions may be fried in ham grease in lieu of bacon grease. Crumbled ham can also be substituted for the bacon to garnish the casserole. For a main dish, add 1 cup cubed ham to the beans before baking. Serve with a tossed salad and French bread for a complete meal.

# MARINATED CARROT SALAD

Makes 2 quarts

This keeps well in the refrigerator for one week. It is great for covered dish affairs.

Cook until done:

**2 pounds carrots, chopped**

Drain and cool. Mix well and add to cut carrots:

**1 ten ounce can tomato soup**
**¾ cup sugar**

**¼ cup vinegar**
**1 teaspoon salt**
**¼ teaspoon dry mustard**
**dash pepper**
**1 tablespoon Worcestershire sauce**
**½ cup oil**

Chop and add to carrot mixture:

**3 small onions**
**1 green pepper**

Chill several hours or overnight.

# SUNSHINE CARROTS

6 to 8 servings

Sliver and boil in water to cover until tender, about 5 minutes:

**1 pound carrots**

Place in a saucepan with cool water to cover:

**peel from one orange**

Boil and drain. Repeat three times with orange peel. In a large bowl, combine carrots and peel. In a saucepan bring to a boil:

**1 cup sugar**
**½ cup water**

Cook for 5 to 10 minutes or until clear and syrupy. Add:

**1 tablespoon butter**

Pour over carrots and refrigerate until next day. Serve cold.

# CREAMY CORN PUDDING

8 servings

Preheat oven to 400°. Beat until light and fluffy:

**4 eggs**

Blend together:

**2 tablespoons cornstarch or flour**
**¼ to ½ cup sugar**

Mix with sugar-cornstarch and combine well with eggs:

**1 teaspoon vanilla**
**¾ cup cream or evaporated milk**
**¾ cup milk**
**1 pound can cream style corn**
**¼ teaspoon salt**

Pour into a 1½ quart baking dish and dot with:

**2 tablespoons butter**

Place dish in a pan of water. Bake for about 50 to 60 minutes or until custard is set.

# PICKLED EGGS

Makes 12

My mother, Mamie Roberson, always served these with the Easter ham. They make a colorful garnish and will add color and flavor to a buffet cold meat tray.

**1 dozen eggs**

Cool, peel, and drop into a quart jar containing:

**2 cups pickled beet juice**

Marinate for 3 days before using to get full benefit from beet color and flavor.

# BAKED GRITS CROCKER

6 to 8 servings

Grits are a traditional Southern dish usually served with sliced ham. This dish can be made the day before. Refrigerate until time to bake.

Preheat oven to 350°. Bring to a boil:

**1 quart milk**

Add:

**1 cup regular grits**
**2 sticks butter**

¼ **teaspoon pepper**
½ **teaspoon salt**

Cook until thick. Remove from heat and beat in:

**6 ounces grated Gruyere cheese**
¼ **cup grated Parmesan cheese**

Pour into a greased casserole and sprinkle on top:

¼ **cup grated Parmesan cheese**

Bake 1 hour.

# SAVORY HOMINY

6 to 8 servings

Serve with broiled ham steak.

Preheat oven to 350°. Beat slightly:

**2 eggs**

Add and continue beating:

**3 cups milk**
**1 cup granulated hominy**

**1 teaspoon salt**
**1½ tablespoons onion juice**
**3 tablespoons finely chopped green pepper**

Pour into a greased casserole and place in a pan of hot water. Bake for 1 to 1½ hours. Stir occasionally during the first part of cooking.

# BAKED PUMPKIN

10 to 12 servings

This is served as a vegetable with a ham dinner.

Preheat oven to 325°. Combine in a large mixing bowl:

**3 tablespoons flour**
**1½ cups sugar**

Add and mix well:

**3 cups cooked pumpkin**
¾ **cup very finely chopped coconut**

**3 eggs, beaten**
½ **teaspoon allspice**
½ **teaspoon pumpkin pie spice**
¼ **teaspoon salt**
½ **teaspoon cinnamon**
**1 ten ounce can evaporated milk**

Grease a 9 by 13 inch baking dish with butter. Spoon in pumpkin mixture. Top with:

½ **cup pecan halves**

Bake until golden, 45 minutes to 1 hour.

# SPINACH SUPREME

6 servings

Preheat oven to 350°. Cook and drain thoroughly:

**2 ten ounce packages frozen chopped spinach**

Mix with:

**½ cup grated Cheddar cheese**
**1 cup sour cream**

**1 eight ounce can tomato sauce**
**1 four ounce can chopped mushrooms**
**2 tablespoons finely minced onion (optional)**

Pour into a casserole dish and top with:

**1 cup grated Cheddar cheese**

Bake 25 minutes.

# SWEET POTATOES WITH APPLES

8 servings

This dish will keep nicely for several days and is good reheated.

Preheat oven to 350°. Boil until done:

**3 pounds sweet potatoes**

Peel and slice. Arrange in a layer in a large casserole dish. Alternate layers of potatoes with:

**1 twenty ounce can unsweetened sliced apples**

Combine in a saucepan over medium heat until sugar is dissolved:

**½ cup orange juice**
**½ cup pineapple juice**
**1 cup brown sugar**
**1 cup white sugar**
**1 teaspoon lemon extract**
**1 tablespoon cornstarch**
**1 teaspoon cinnamon**

Pour over potato-apple layers. Dot with:

**2 tablespoons butter**

Bake for 30 minutes.

# GLAZED SWEET POTATOES

Preheat oven to 350°. In a greased casserole or pie plate slice:

**4 to 6 cooked sweet potatoes, peeled**

Sprinkle with:

**dash cinnamon**
**dash nutmeg**

Pour over this:

**½ cup dark corn syrup**
**½ to ¾ cup orange juice**

Dot with:

**2 tablespoons butter**

Bake for about 30 to 40 minutes, until potatoes are well glazed. For an alternate glaze combine 1 cup brown sugar with ¼ cup water and bake. Another suggestion is to glaze potatoes with honey.

---

## SWEET POTATO FLUFF

---

8 servings

Katherine Godwin, wife of Governor Mills E. Godwin, Jr., of Virginia, usually serves ham freshly cooked and sliced. She quite often serves this with sliced ham. It is a good dish to prepare a day before or earlier if desired. For a different way to serve this, mound on pineapple slices or stuff into orange shells.

Preheat oven to 375°. Boil, peel and beat with electric mixer:

**6 medium sweet potatoes**

Add, while potatoes are warm:

**½ stick butter**

Blend and beat in:

**¾ cup sugar**

Stir in:

**1 eight ounce can crushed pineapple**
**1 cup white raisins**
**cinnamon to taste**

Pour into a buttered casserole dish and bake until hot. You can melt on top enough to cover the dish:

**marshmallows**

---

## OLD-FASHIONED POTATO SALAD

---

4 servings

In a large mixing bowl combine:

**2 cups diced cooked potatoes**
**2 hard cooked eggs, diced**

In a small bowl combine:

**½ cup chopped celery**
**½ cup** *Homemade Sweet Cucumber Pickle,* chopped

**½ cup mayonnaise**
**1 tablespoon finely minced onion**
**1 teaspoon prepared mustard**
**salt and pepper to taste**
**1 tablespoon pickle juice**

Pour over potatoes and blend well. Garnish with:

**paprika**

# SOUR CREAM RICE CASSEROLE

10 to 12 servings

This can be made ahead and baked just before serving. It is also good reheated. This is a special dish to accompany ham—grand for a crowd! Put in a pot with a tight cover (greasing rim of pot with butter will prevent boiling over):

**1 cup uncooked long grain rice**
**2 cups water**
**1 teaspoon salt**
**1 tablespoon vinegar**
**1 teaspoon peanut oil**

Bring to a boil and turn off the heat, leaving the lid on tight. Let set for 45 minutes on burner of stove. Preheat oven to 400°. In an ungreased casserole, alternate 2 layers of cooked rice with 2 layers of:

**1 pound sharp cheese, grated**
**2 tablespoons sugar**
**dash crushed red pepper**

Pour over casserole:

**1 pint sour cream**

Sprinkle with:

**2 tablespoons toasted bread crumbs**

Dot with:

**2 tablespoons butter**

Bake for 25 to 30 minutes, or until lightly brown. For a superior sour cream, make your own: in a pan of warm water place one pint carton of whipping cream. Pour 2 tablespoons of vinegar into the carton and stir. Leave for about 1 hour.

# BAKED TOMATO HALVES

8 servings

Preheat oven to 375°. Cut in half through the equator:

**4 tomatoes**

Brush this mixture on cut side of halves:

**1 teaspoon mayonnaise**

**dash basil**
**dash Worcestershire sauce**
**dash Tabasco sauce**
**dash sugar**

Place in shallow dish with ¼ inch water. Bake for 30 minutes until brown. Serve these with *Chicken and Ham Divan.*

# TOMATO PUDDING

10 to 12 servings

Preheat oven to 375°. In a saucepan put:

**1 thirty-two ounce can tomatoes**

Cook until tomatoes fall to pieces. Add:

**1½ cups sugar**
**¼ pound saltine crackers, finely crumbled**
**½ stick butter**

Let simmer until all saltines disappear. Place in a baking dish and bake for 15 to 20 minutes.

# FIRST LADY'S RUBY RED GRAPEFRUIT

4 to 6 servings

Betty Ford, former First Lady of the United States, graciously sent me her favorite accompaniment for sliced Virginia ham. This is quick cooking, and follows the Southern tradition of accompanying ham with another meat.

Peel and section:

**2 ruby red grapefruit**

Be sure to squeeze all juice from the membranes into a saucepan. Add and mix well:

**½ cup whole cranberry sauce**
**1 tablespoon honey**

**¼ teaspoon cloves**
**¼ teaspoon salt**

Bring to a boil and stir in grapefruit sections.

Cut in serving size pieces:

**1 frying chicken**

Brown chicken in:

**3 tablespoons butter or margarine**

Place chicken in a shallow baking dish. Baste with grapefruit sauce. Bake for about 45 minutes, basting frequently. Serve chicken with remaining grapefruit sauce.

# DESSERTS

## LEMON CHESS PIE

6 to 8 servings

Preheat oven to 350°. Combine in a mixing bowl:

  **2 cups sugar**
  **2 tablespoons corn meal**
  **1 tablespoon flour**

Add one at a time, beating well after each:

  **4 eggs**

Add:

  **¼ cup lemon juice**
  **4 teaspoons grated lemon rind**
  **¼ cup milk**
  **¼ cup melted butter**

Mix well and pour into:

  **1 unbaked pie shell**

Bake for 45 minutes.

## RASPBERRY COMPOTE

4 servings

Fresh fruits or frozen fruits combined make a light tasty dessert to accompany a ham dinner. You will find these refreshing!

  Mix:

  **1 ten ounce package thawed frozen raspberries with juice**
  **1 fresh peach, cut up**
  **1 fresh plum, cut up (optional)**
  **1 cup sour cream**

Place fruit in parfait glasses or compotes and serve.

## FRUIT AND MELON PARFAIT

4 servings

Combine:

  **cantaloupe and/or honeydew-melon balls**
  **fresh strawberries and blueberries**
  **fresh peaches, cut up**

Place in parfait glasses or compotes. Place a scoop of lime or orange sherbert on top. Pour about ¼ cup ginger ale into each parfait, depending on size of parfait. Top with a strawberry or cherry and a sprig of mint to serve. For a buffet brunch, place in a large crystal bowl and let guests help themselves.

## GRAND MARNIER FRUIT COMPOTE

Marinate in Grand Marnier liqueur for several hours or overnight in refrigerator, desired proportions of:

**pineapple chunks**

**sliced bananas**
**seeded grapes**

Arrange in crystal compote on a buffet table or serve in individual compotes.

## ORANGES GUSTAV

8 servings

These candied oranges make an unusual dessert that looks pretty and tastes delicious.

Cut in half crosswise, remove core and seeds from:

**4 whole oranges**

Bring to boil in a saucepan:

**3 cups sugar**
**3 cups water**

Add the oranges, cover saucepan, reduce heat to simmer and cook for 1 hour or longer, until oranges are very tender when pierced with a fork and can be easily eaten. Cool. Store in syrup. Drain:

**1 ten ounce package frozen strawberries**

Blend the strawberry juice with:

**2 tablespoons cornstarch**

Cook until clear and thickened. Cool and add the strawberries. Any extra syrup may be frozen for future use. To serve, fill the cavity in the orange halves with strawberries and a little syrup. Top with:

**whipped cream**
**slivered candied ginger**

## PINEAPPLE PUDDING

6 servings

Preheat oven to 350°. Mix the following ingredients:

**5 slices bread, broken up**
**3 eggs, beaten**

**pinch salt**
**1 sixteen ounce can crushed pineapple**
**½ cup sugar**
**1 stick margarine**

Bake for 30 minutes.

# PEANUT PIE

8 servings

Prepare:

> single 9 inch deep dish pastry
> shell, baked or 2 regular
> pastry shells, baked

In large mixing bowl dissolve:

> 1 envelope plain gelatin
> ¼ cup milk

Add:

> ½ cup peanut butter
> 1 four ounce package cream
> cheese

> 1 cup sifted confectioners sugar
> ½ teaspoon vanilla extract

Fold in:

> 1 nine ounce carton prepared
> whipped topping

Pour into prepared pie shells and refrigerate overnight before serving. You can freeze this pie and allow a few minutes to thaw before serving. Garnish with crushed peanuts. This pie is also delicious in a graham cracker crust.

# NELL ASBURY'S BUTTERSCOTCH PIE

Preheat oven to 400°. Combine:

> 2 cups brown sugar
> 5 tablespoons flour
> 6 tablespoons butter

Beat:

> 3 egg yolks

Add:

> 2 cups milk

Pour into brown sugar mixture and cook until very thick, stirring constantly. Cool. Add and stir well:

> 1½ teaspoons vanilla
> pinch salt

Pour into:

> single 9 inch baked pie crust

Make meringue; whip until stiff:

> 3 egg whites

Add and blend:

> ½ cup sugar

Pour over pie mixture and bake for about 12 to 15 minutes or until lightly browned.

# SWEET POTATO PIE

8 servings

Preheat oven to 400°. Prepare:

> 1 deep dish pie crust

Boil, peel and mash:

> about 1 pound sweet potatoes
> or 1 pound can

Combine:

> ¾ cup evaporated milk

¼ cup water

Combine with:

1 cup sugar
½ stick butter
½ teaspoon cinnamon
¼ teaspoon nutmeg

1 tablespoon vanilla
2 eggs, beaten
dash salt

Pour into unbaked pie shell. Bake at 400° for 10 minutes, then 350° for about 30 to 40 minutes or until inserted knife blade comes out clean.

## ELIZABETH'S SWEET POTATO PUDDING

6 servings

Preheat oven to 375°. Peel, grate and place in a bowl:

4 medium sweet potatoes

Add:

1 thirteen ounce can evaporated milk

In another bowl combine then mix with sweet potatoes:

2 cups sugar
2 tablespoons flour
3 eggs, beaten
dash salt
½ stick butter, melted
1 teaspoon vanilla
½ teaspoon lemon extract

Pour into a greased baking dish and bake for about 40 minutes or until brown. Add ½ cup coconut or crushed pineapple to the mixture to make a nice variation.

## STRAWBERRY BAVARIAN MARCELLE

6 servings

This is heavenly!

Put in a small bowl:

½ cup cold water

Sprinkle on water:

2 three ounce packages unflavored gelatin

Set aside to let soften. In top of double boiler beat:

6 egg yolks

Add:

¾ cup sugar

⅛ teaspoon salt

Beat until lemon colored and thick. Gradually blend in:

2¼ cups milk

Cook over hot water stirring constantly until custard coats metal spoon. Remove from heat and stir in softened gelatin and:

3 teaspoons vanilla

Cook, stirring occasionally to prevent formation of skim on the surface. Chill until the mixture thickens to the consistency of unbeaten egg whites. Beat until stiff:

**1 cup whipping cream**

Fold this into egg mixture. Remove two cups of this custard to another mixing bowl. Mash and fold in:

**1 pint fresh strawberries**

Stir in:

**1 teaspoon freshly grated lemon rind**

Pour half of the vanilla custard into a 6-cup mold. Chill until set. Pour half of the strawberry custard over the vanilla. Chill until set. Repeat. Chill several hours. Unmold onto serving platter or compote. Spoon *Marcelle Sauce* over individual servings.

## MARCELLE SAUCE

Combine the following ingredients and allow mixture to stand in refrigerator for at least an hour. Serve over *Strawberry Bavarian*:

**1 pint strawberries, cut in half**
**1 tablespoon freshly grated orange rind**

**1 teaspoon freshly grated lemon rind**
**¼ cup brown sugar**
**¼ cup sweet white wine (Sherry, Port or Muscatel)**
**1 tablespoon Kirsch liqueur**

## MARTHA'S BOURBON ON A CLOUD

6 servings

In the top of a double boiler blend:

**½ cup sugar**
**1 envelope unflavored gelatin**

Stir in:

**3 slightly beaten egg yolks**

Slowly blend in:

**¾ cup bourbon**

Place double boiler top over simmering water and cook, stirring constantly, about 10 minutes or until mixture thickens slightly. In a small bowl, beat until foamy:

**3 egg whites**

Add gradually:

**¼ cup sugar**

Beat until soft peaks form. Gradually fold bourbon mixture into egg whites. Chill. Fold in:

**1 cup whipping cream, whipped**

Split in half:

**12 ladyfingers**

Line a 4 cup mold with ladyfingers, the cut sides outside. A springform pan is nice because you can remove the sides and show off this pretty dessert. Pour into cream mixture mold and chill at least 6 hours or overnight.

# LOVELACE SHERRY ICEBOX CAKE

16 servings

This is a light dessert to follow a heavy meal or accompany a luncheon. Cook in a double boiler until thickened:

**6 egg yolks**
**1 cup dry or cream sherry**
**¾ cup sugar**

Soak:

**2 envelopes of gelatin**
**½ cup milk**

Add to first mixture while it is still warm. Cool, and fold in:

**6 egg whites, beaten stiffly**

Whip:

**1½ pints whipping cream**

Add gradually:

**¾ cup sugar**

Fold into egg white mixture. Break into bite-size pieces and drop into mixture:

**1 large angel-food cake**

Pour into large oiled angel cake pan. Refrigerate for 10 to 12 hours. Unmold and ice with:

**1 cup whipping cream, whipped**

Refrigerate until serving time.

# COUSIN SANDRA'S SUNDAE CAKE

Layer in 9 by 13 inch oblong dish:

**2 cups graham cracker crumbs**
**1 stick butter, melted**

Beat at medium speed for 15 minutes:

**2 eggs**
**2 sticks butter**
**2 cups powdered sugar**
**1 teaspoon vanilla**

Spread over graham cracker crumbs.

Layer on top:

**2 or 3 cut bananas, sprinkled**
**with a little lemon juice**
**1 four ounce can crushed**
**pineapple, drained**
**1 sixteen ounce container**
**whipped topping**

Garnish with strawberries or cherries and nuts. Refrigerate until firm and serve.

# COBBLESTONE COFFEE CAKE

12 servings

This is a coffee cake that is out of this world. The recipe originated with Mrs. Evelyn Howell, home economics teacher at Greensboro College. This cake will make 25 to 30 bite size servings, which is perfect for a morning coffee featuring ham biscuits and fresh fruit. For a special brunch, serve with *Fried Apple Rings* and *Ham Brunch Casserole*.

In a large mixing bowl, dissolve and cool to lukewarm:

**¾ cup boiling water**
**½ cup shortening**
**¼ cup plus two tablespoons sugar**
**¾ teaspoon salt**

Dissolve in another small bowl:

**1 package granular yeast**
**¼ cup lukewarm water**

Stir into yeast mixture:

**1 egg, well beaten**

Stir yeast mixture into the shortening-sugar mixture; then stir in until well blended:

**3½ cups sifted all purpose flour**

The mixture does not look workable. Grease the top of the dough and store in the refrigerator for at least 3 hours. It can be stored, however, for several days before using. Preheat oven to 350°. Shape the dough into small walnut-size balls. Dip the balls into:

**3 ounces melted butter**

Dip balls into a mixture of:

**1 cup white sugar**
**2½ teaspoons cinnamon**

Grease a tube pan and place balls on top of each other like marbles until all are used. Let rise until double in bulk, about 2 hours. Bake for 45 minutes.

# BRIDE'S DESSERT

8 servings

This is a lovely dessert you make a day ahead.

Beat together in a small bowl until soft peaks form:

**3 egg whites**
**¼ teaspoon salt**

Gradually beat into egg whites until stiff peaks form:

**¾ cup sugar**

Fold in:

**¾ cup fine chocolate wafer crumbs**

Add and stir:

**½ cup chopped pecans or walnuts**
**½ teaspoon vanilla**

Spread evenly in a 9-inch pie plate lightly greased with butter or margarine. Bake 30 to 35 minutes in a 325° oven. Cool thoroughly.

Whip until soft peaks form:

**1 cup whipping cream**

Add:

**1 tablespoon sugar**

Spread over cooled pie mixture. Garnish with:

**2 tablespoons shaved bitter chocolate**

Chill 24 hours before serving.

---

## TEN MINUTE CHOCOLATE CHESS PIE

---

8 servings

Preheat oven to 350°. Melt in a small saucepan and cool:

**½ stick butter or margarine**

Combine in mixing bowl along with cooled butter or margarine:

**3½ tablespoons cocoa**

**1½ cups sugar**
**pinch salt**
**1 six-ounce can evaporated milk**
**2 eggs, beaten**
**1 teaspoon vanilla**

Pour into:

**1 unbaked pie shell**

Bake for 45 minutes.

# CASSEROLES

Pembroke, 1701

A tasty ham casserole highlights an afternoon picnic on the spacious lawn of Pembroke plantation, located on the Nansemond River in Suffolk, Virginia. Mr. and Mrs. Frank M. Warrington, the present owners, acquired Pembroke in 1940 and restored it in authentic eighteenth century detail.

Pembroke, named for the Earl of Pembroke, was built in 1701 by an eccentric sea captain known as Captain Jack. He disappeared mysteriously leaving his overseer, Patrick Wilkinson, in possession of the plantation. Names and dates carved in the old brick attest to the mark left on Pembroke by three wars: the Revolution, the War of 1812, and the War Between the States. The interior was burned during the War of 1812.

During the War Between the States the family of James Hunter Godwin owned Pembroke. Many slaves had left the Godwins and joined Lieutenant Roy of the Union Army. When he brought his troops down the Nansemond River in the spring of 1865, some of the slaves who had lived there previously pleaded for him not to fire on Pembroke. In all probability, this saved the house from being severely burned or shelled. The northern soldiers did, however, come ashore and help themselves to whatever they wanted...including a raid on the Godwins' smokehouse in which they took the family's cherished Virginia hams.

Pembroke is one of the two remaining U-shaped homes in Virginia today. It is a story and a half in height and is built of old English bricks that are laid in Flemish bond. It is listed in the Historic American Buildings Survey as "possessing historic and architectural interest and as being worthy of most careful preservation for the benefit of future generations."

# HAM CASSEROLES

Casserole cookery is a centuries old method of preparing food. People have been cooking combinations of foods ever since they discovered that earthenware could stand direct heat from the fire.

The word casserole reportedly means "little pot," and probably evolved from the centuries old French regional dish, *cassoulet*. This is a hearty concoction of dried white beans and meat that after a long period of slow cooking develops into a rich stew. A green salad and piece of fresh fruit complete this provincial meal.

Ham casseroles range from the breakfast *Mix and Bake Egg and Ham Montgomery*, which is mixed in the casserole dish, to the elegant dinner party dish, *Ham and Chicken Divan*. This is a treat your guests will appreciate.

Casseroles are convenient because they can be made ahead of time, baked and served in the same container. Be economical: make use of those leftover pieces of ham by selecting and preparing a tasty ham casserole for your family or guests. For a dinner menu, serve:

*Ham and Chicken Divan*
*Baked Tomato Halves*
*Holiday Cranberry Mold*
*Sally Lunn*
*Lemon Chess Pie*

## HAM-ASPARAGUS ROLLS

4 servings

Preheat oven to 350°.

Cook until tender:

**16 stalks fresh asparagus or 1 ten ounce package frozen asparagus or 1 pound can asparagus**

Prepare:

**4 thin slices cooked ham**

Wrap 1 slice of ham around 4 asparagus spears. Repeat for each slice. Place folded side down in a lightly greased casserole dish. Top each ham roll with one half of:

**2 slices Swiss cheese**

Bake for 15 minutes. If you prefer a cheese sauce, omit the Swiss cheese and pour *Sour Cream-Cheese Sauce* over the casserole before baking.

# SOUR CREAM-CHEESE SAUCE

Melt in a saucepan:

**4 tablespoons butter or margarine**

Stir in:

**¼ cup flour**

Add gradually, stirring constantly:

**1½ cups milk**

Cook until mixture thickens, then add to sauce and stir until cheese melts:

**1 cup grated Cheddar or Swiss cheese**
**1 cup sour cream**

# HAM SKILLET CASSEROLE

This top of the stove casserole is quick and absolutely delicious. Even if your taste does not fancy squash, you will love this dish.

Place in a skillet:

**1 chopped onion**
**1 ten ounce package of squash or 4 medium size yellow squash cut into pieces**
**1 ten ounce package frozen cauliflower or 1 small head cauliflower, broken into buds**
**½ cup water**
**2 tablespoons butter**

Steam until tender. Add:

**1 cup cubed ham**

Steam for a few minutes. Cover casserole with:

**1 eight ounce package grated Mozzarella cheese**

After cheese melts, arrange around skillet:

**1 tomato, cut into wedges**
**1 pepper, cut into strips**

Steam for a few more minutes, then serve at once.

# SPEEDY HAM AND BROCCOLI DIVAN

4 to 6 servings

This is a real quickie and so convenient for the working woman. This is good served with *Cranberry Salad with Sour Cream.*

Preheat oven to 375°. Toast, cut into strips and arrange in a baking dish:

**4 slices bread**

Cook, drain, and layer over toast:

**2 ten ounce packages frozen broccoli**

Arrange over broccoli:

**½ to ¾ pound cooked ham, sliced**

Mix:

**1 ten ounce can Cheddar Cheese soup**
**2 tablespoons prepared mustard**
**½ teaspoon steak sauce**
**1 tablespoon milk**

Pour over ham. Bake for 20 minutes.

# FANTASTIC HAM AND CABBAGE DINNER

8 servings

This is a complete meal when served with *Stuffed Red Apples* and *Old-Fashioned Spoon Bread.*

Preheat oven to 350°. In bottom of oblong casserole dish place:

**2 to 3 center slices cooked ham**

Alternate layers of:

**1 small head cabbage, sliced**
**4 to 6 medium potatoes, sliced**
**1 cup cream of mushroom soup diluted with 2 tablespoons milk**

Top with:

**¼ cup bread crumbs or wheat germ or croutons**

Cover and bake about 1 hour until done.

# CHEESY HAM-CARROT CASSEROLE

6 servings

Serve with the salad *Tart Cherry Delight* for a complete meal.

Preheat oven to 350°. In a saucepan melt:

**2 tablespoons margarine**

Add and cook for about 1 minute, stirring constantly:

2 **tablespoons flour**

Stir in:

2 **cups milk**

Cook until well blended, then add:

1 **cup grated sharp cheese**

Stir until cheese melts and sauce is thickened. Alternate layers in a 1½ to 2 quart casserole dish:

1 **large onion, sliced**
4 **carrots, sliced**
5 **potatoes, sliced**
6 **slices cooked ham**

Pour cheese sauce over all. Cover and bake for 1 hour.

## HAM AND CAULIFLOWER BROOKS

6 servings

Preheat oven to 375°. Cook in salted boiling water until almost done:

1 **head cauliflower**

Drain, run cold water on cauliflower, then break into flowerets. In bottom of a greased casserole, alternate layers of flowerets with layers of:

2 **cups chopped cooked Country ham**

Dot top with:

2 **tablespoons butter**

For a sauce, combine:

1½ **cups sour cream**
¼ **cup chopped onions**

2 **egg yolks, slightly beaten**
⅛ **teaspoon nutmeg**
⅛ **teaspoon mace**
1½ **teaspoons paprika**
¼ **teaspoon pepper**

Mix well and pour over casserole. Cover and bake for 25 to 30 minutes. Remove cover, top with:

¾ **cup grated Cheddar cheese**

Brown slightly and serve. Fresh mushrooms may be added to this recipe. Sauté them in butter first, then add between layers of cauliflower and ham. This casserole can be made the day before and baked just before serving.

# CREAMY HAM-CAULIFLOWER CASSEROLE

6 servings

Preheat oven to 350°. Break into buds to yield about 4 cups:

**1 medium head cauliflower (about 2 pounds)**

Cook, covered, in boiling water until tender (10 to 12 minutes). Drain. Sauté:

**1 three ounce can sliced mushrooms, drained, or 4 ounces sliced fresh mushrooms**
**1 teaspoon butter**
**2 tablespoons water**
**½ teaspoon salt**

Combine mushroom mixture with:

**2 cups chopped cooked ham**

In medium saucepan, melt:

**4 tablespoons butter or margarine**

Stir in:

**¼ cup flour**

Add:

**1 cup milk**

Cook and stir until mixture thickens and bubbles. Add:

**1 cup cubed sharp cheese**
**1 cup dairy sour cream**

Stir till cheese melts. Combine with ham mixture and cauliflower. Turn into a 2 quart casserole. Sauté:

**1 cup soft bread crumbs**

In:

**2 tablespoons melted butter**

Sprinkle crumbs over top. Bake, covered, 40 minutes or until hot.

# SCALLOPED CELERY WITH HAM

6 servings

Serve this as an accompaniment to roast beef, chicken or turkey.

Preheat oven to 375°. Grease a 1½ quart casserole. Diagonally cut in ½ inch pieces and boil until tender in just enough water to cover:

**4 cups celery**

In a saucepan over medium heat melt:

**2 tablespoons butter**

Stir in:

**2 tablespoons flour**

Gradually add:

**2 cups milk**

Stir constantly until sauce is thick and smooth. Add drained celery and:

**½ cup finely chopped Country ham**

Pour into casserole and top with:

**½ cup buttered bread crumbs**
**½ cup chopped pecans**

Bake for 20 minutes until lightly browned.

# CHEESE AND BROCCOLI DISH

6 servings

Make this ahead for a hurry-up dinner. Cut with a doughnut cutter:

**12 slices white bread**

Set bread circles aside, fit the scraps of bread in the bottom of a 13 by 9 by 2 inch baking dish.

Layer over bread in this order:

- **¾ pound sharp American cheese, grated (save about ¼ cup to sprinkle on finished casserole)**
- **1 ten ounce package frozen chopped broccoli, cooked and drained or 1 pound can asparagus spears, drained**
- **2 cups diced cooked ham**

Arrange bread doughnuts and holes on top. Combine and pour over casserole:

- **6 eggs, slightly beaten**
- **3½ cups milk**
- **2 tablespoons instant or freshly minced onion**
- **½ teaspoon salt (omit if ham is salty)**
- **¼ teaspoon dry mustard**

Cover and refrigerate at least 6 hours or overnight.

Bake uncovered at 325° for 55 minutes. For a pretty finish, sprinkle with shredded cheese 5 minutes before end of baking time. Let stand 10 minutes before cutting into squares for serving. Garnish with:

**chopped fresh parsley**

# HAM AND CHEESE CASSEROLE

6 to 8 servings

Doris Miller, wife of the former Attorney General of Virginia, Andrew Miller, sent me this tasty macaroni recipe.

Preheat oven to 300°. Make cheese sauce by blending over medium heat:

- **2 tablespoons butter or margarine**
- **2 tablespoons flour**

Slowly add and stir:

**1 cup milk**

Add:

- **dash salt**
- **dash red pepper**
- **½ teaspoon dry mustard**
- **1 cup shredded or cubed mild cheese**

Stir until cheese melts and add:

- **1 cup cubed cooked ham**
- **2 cups cooked macaroni or noodles**

Blend mixture and pour into a greased casserole. Cover with:

**cracker crumbs (optional)**

Bake for about 30 minutes.

# PARMESAN HAM BAKE

4 servings

This makes a good supper served with a baked potato and green bean casserole.

Preheat oven to 350°. Place in an oven-proof dish:

> **one pound package of ⅛ inch sliced breakfast Country ham or a 1 inch thick slice of raw smoked ham**

Pour over the ham:

> **1 cup mashed undrained canned tomatoes**

Sprinkle with a little:

> **pepper**
> **oregano**

Cover the dish. Bake until ham is tender, about ¾ hour. Uncover the last 15 minutes of cooking. After uncovering, sprinkle over the ham:

> **¼ cup grated Parmesan cheese**

# EASY MACARONI AND CHEESE HAM DINNER

4 servings

Preheat oven to 375°. Prepare according to package directions:

> **1 eight ounce box packaged macaroni and cheese dinner**

Brown on both sides if cooked or fry until done if uncooked:

> **1 ham steak**

Mix into the cheese dinner:

> **¼ cup red wine**

**1 four ounce can mushrooms, drained**

Pour the mixed cheese and macaroni into a casserole dish. Place the browned ham steak on top. Place in corners of casserole:

> **4 tomato wedges**

Sprinkle with:

> **¼ cup grated Cheddar cheese**

Bake until bubbly, 15 to 20 minutes.

# HAM TETRAZZINI

6 to 8 servings

This is good for a quick company casserole.

Preheat oven to 375°. Saute until transparent:

¼ **cup finely chopped onion**
½ **cup melted butter**

Add and cook until tender:

2 **cups sliced fresh mushrooms**

Blend in:

5 **tablespoons plus**
1 **teaspoon flour**

Stir in and continue stirring and cooking until smooth and thickened:

2 **cups milk**
2 **cups half and half**

Add:

dash garlic powder
dash pepper

Mix together and put in bottom of a 2 quart shallow baking dish:

½ **cup shredded Parmesan cheese**
1 **seven ounce package spaghetti, cooked**

Cover spaghetti-cheese mixture with alternate layers of mushroom sauce and:

2 **cups thinly sliced ham pieces**

End with sauce and sprinkle over top:

¼ **cup shredded Parmesan cheese**

Bake until bubbly around edges of dish and brown on top, about 20 to 25 minutes.

## HAM-CHICKEN CASSEROLE

6 servings

This recipe can be prepared early in the morning. Cover and refrigerate until 1 hour before oven time to allow it to reach room temperature. Serve with French style green beans and *Curried Pineapple Rings.*

Preheat oven to 375°. Cover bottom of 12 by 7 by 2 inch baking dish with:

6 **to 8 thin slices Smithfield or Country ham**

Top with deboned, halved:

3 **chicken breasts**

Dot chicken with:

salt
pepper
paprika
butter

Pour over top:

1 **ten ounce can cream of mushroom soup**

Bake uncovered for 45 minutes.

# COMPANY CASSEROLE

6 to 8 servings

Preheat oven to 350°. Layer the bottom of a large baking dish with:

**6 to 8 slices cooked Virginia ham**

Cut into serving pieces and salt lightly to taste:

**1 frying chicken, about
3½ pounds**

Pour over the chicken:

**1 ten ounce can cream of
mushroom soup
½ cup sour cream
¼ cup Sauterne wine**

Sprinkle over casserole:

**1 cup packaged dressing or
seasoned bread crumbs**

Bake until chicken is golden brown, about 1 hour. Serve with buttered broccoli and *Apricot-Banana Mold Matthew.*

# HAM AND CHICKEN BAKE BONNER

6 to 8 servings

Preheat oven to 350°. Sauté:

**½ cup diced onion
½ cup diced celery
4 tablespoons margarine**

Blend in:

**4 tablespoons flour**

Combine and add to flour, stirring constantly until it boils:

**1½ cups chicken broth
1½ cups milk**

Add:

**1½ to 2 cups diced cooked ham
2 cups diced cooked chicken
1 four ounce can sliced
mushrooms, drained
dash pepper**

Heat through and pour into an ungreased baking dish. Top with:

**1 eight ounce can refrigerator
biscuits**

Bake for 30 to 40 minutes or until biscuits are done. Serve with a congealed salad for a complete meal.

# PARTY CHICKEN AND HAM

8 servings

Preheat oven to 300°. Bone and halve:

**4 chicken breasts**

Season lightly with:

red pepper
garlic salt
celery salt

Line bottom of casserole dish with:

**8 slices cooked Smithfield ham**

Wrap each half chicken breast in one of:

**8 slices bacon**

Place chicken on ham. Combine and spread over the dish:

**1 ten ounce can cream of mushroom soup**
**1 cup sour cream**
**¼ cup sherry, optional**
**1 four ounce can mushrooms, drained**

Bake 2 to 2½ hours or until chicken is very tender. This dish makes its own sauce to accompany the chicken.

## SCALLOPED EGGPLANT AND HAM

4 servings

Preheat oven to 350°. Pare:

**1 medium to large eggplant**

Cut into 1 inch cubes. Cook in boiling salted water until just tender, about 8 minutes. Drain. Add:

**1 beaten egg**
**2 tablespoons melted butter**

**1 small onion, chopped**
**½ cup milk**
**1 cup dry bread crumbs**
**½ cup ham bits or ground ham**

Place in greased casserole, top with:

**½ cup grated Cheddar cheese**

Bake 30 minutes.

## CREAMED ONIONS WITH HAM

8 servings

This is a vegetable dish to accompany the main course. It is delicious served with roast beef.

Preheat oven to 375°. Grease a 1 quart casserole dish. Cook in boiling slightly salted water until tender:

**16 small white onions**

Drain. Melt over medium heat:

**2 tablespoons butter**

Stir in:

**2 tablespoons flour**

Add, stirring constantly until smooth and slightly thickened:

**2 scant cups milk**

Place onions in prepared casserole and pour cream sauce over them. Top with:

**½ cup minced cooked ham**
**½ cup buttered bread crumbs**

Bake for about 20 minutes or until lightly browned and bubbly.

# HOT SWISS POTATO AND HAM CASSEROLE

4 to 6 servings

Preheat oven to 350°. Make sauce by melting on low heat:

**2 tablespoons butter**

Add and stir well:

**2 tablespoons flour**

Gradually add, stirring constantly:

**2 cups milk**
**1 teaspoon salt (omit if ham is salty)**

Turn heat up to medium and boil 1 minute until well thickened. In a 2½ quart buttered casserole dish, alternate sauce with layers of:

**4 large potatoes, cooked and sliced**
**2 cups (approx.) cubed cooked ham**
**1½ cups diced green onion**
**2 cups shredded Swiss cheese**

Top casserole with:

**¼ cup buttered bread crumbs**

Bake 15 to 20 minutes until cheese melts and casserole is bubbly. Serve with tossed salad and *Corn Sticks* for a complete meal.

# CHICKEN AND HAM DIVAN

8 servings

This is a great casserole for guests. Serve with *Baked Tomato Halves* for a colorful plate.

Preheat oven to 350°. Butter an oblong casserole dish. Partially cook and drain, then place in the buttered dish:

**3 ten ounce packages frozen broccoli spears**

Place on top of the broccoli:

**6 thin slices cooked Smithfield or Country ham**

Cover ham with:

**5 to 6 cooked chicken breast halves, sliced**

Mix and spread over the casserole:

**2 ten ounce cans cream of chicken soup**
**1 cup mayonnaise**
**2 tablespoons lemon juice**
**1 tablespoon Worcestershire sauce**
**dash Tabasco**
**¼ teaspoon curry powder**

Top with:

**1 cup grated cheese**
**1 cup buttered bread crumbs**

Bake covered until it bubbles, about 15 minutes. Make your own bread crumbs by putting 4 slices of dry bread in the blender and pushing the grate button.

# SMITHFIELD HAM AND CRABMEAT DELUXE

6 servings

Preheat oven to 350°. Cover bottom of a 12 by 7 by 2 inch baking dish with:

**6 or 7 slices Smithfield or Country ham**

Top with:

**1 pound crabmeat**

Dot with:

**1 stick butter
salt
pepper**

Cover and bake for 30 minutes. If you want to serve more guests, just continue another layer of ham and crab seasoned with butter, salt, and pepper.

# MIX AND BAKE EGG AND HAM MONTGOMERY

4 servings

This is easy because it can be mixed ahead and cooked in the same dish. Mix this dish several hours before baking or the night before and let stand in the refrigerator. It freezes well, and is great for brunch or a light supper with English muffins.

Mix together in a baking dish:

**6 eggs, beaten
2 cups whole milk**

**½ pound or 1 cup chopped cooked ham
½ cup chopped green pepper (optional)
½ cup chopped onion (optional)
½ cup chopped mushrooms (optional)
2 slices bread with crust removed, broken up
½ cup grated Cheddar cheese**

Bake at 350°, covered, for 45 minutes.

# HAM AND POTATO CASSEROLE

4 servings

Preheat oven to 350°. Heat in a saucepan:

**1 ten ounce can cream of celery soup**

Add:

**6 ounces sharp cheese, grated
½ cup sour cream**

Stir in:

**2 cups cubed potatoes, cooked
2 cups (approx.) cubed cooked ham**

Pour into 1½ quart casserole. Top with:

**½ cup bread crumbs**

Bake for 30 minutes.

# CHEESY HAM STUFFED PEPPERS

4 servings

Preheat oven to 350°. Cut stems, ribs and seeds from:

**4 large green peppers**

Blanch peppers in boiling water for about 5 minutes. Do not overcook. Remove, turn upside down to drain. Meanwhile, combine:

**1 cup finely chopped or ground cooked ham**
**1 teaspoon onion flakes or ¼ cup finely chopped onion**
**2 cups cooked rice**
**1 large tomato, peeled and diced**

**or ½ cup drained canned tomatoes**
**½ ten ounce can Cheddar cheese soup**
**¼ teaspoon pepper**
**dash salt (omit if Country ham is used)**

Stuff peppers with ham filling and place in a shallow baking dish. Bake 25 to 30 minutes. Mix rest of soup with:

**¼ cup milk**

Heat and use as a cheese sauce for peppers when served.

# GARDEN STUFFED PEPPERS

4 servings

If you freeze vegetables from a summer garden, this is a nice dish to prepare because you will have almost everything in your freezer ready to be utilized.

Preheat oven to 350°. Combine in a mixing bowl:

**2 cups chopped cooked ham**
**½ cup cooked corn**
**½ cup chopped cooked tomatoes**
**2 slices finely crumbled bread**
**1 egg, beaten**
**1 medium onion, chopped**
**¼ cup grated sharp cheese**

Cut stems, core and seeds from:

**4 large green peppers**

Stuff the peppers with ham mixture and place in a casserole dish. Bake for 15 minutes. Meanwhile make sauce; combine in a saucepan:

**½ cup drained canned tomatoes**
**¼ cup tomato juice**
**1½ teaspoons sugar**
**2 teaspoons cornstarch**

Simmer for 15 minutes. Pour over stuffed peppers and continue baking the peppers 15 minutes longer. Top with:

**sliced Mozzarella cheese**

Return to oven to melt cheese. For a quick sauce use 1 eight ounce can of tomato sauce.

# HAM AND POTATO STUFFED PEPPERS

4 servings

Preheat oven to 350°. Remove the stems, ribs and seeds from:

**4 green peppers**

Drop peppers in boiling water and cook for about 5 minutes until just tender. Do not overcook. Turn upside down and drain on paper towel. Mix well:

**1 cup ground cooked ham**

**2 cups cooked mashed potatoes**
**1 teaspoon onion flakes or minced onion**
**1 teaspoon parsley**
**1 teaspoon oregano**
**1 egg, beaten**
**½ teaspoon pepper**

Stuff the green peppers with the mixture. Place in an aluminum foil lined dish and bake 20 to 25 minutes until thoroughly heated through.

# POTATOES AND VIRGINIA HAM AU GRATIN

6 to 8 servings

Consider this dish hale and hearty!

Preheat oven to 350°. Sauté until golden:

**½ cup chopped onions**
**¼ cup chopped green peppers (optional)**

Combine in a saucepan and cook over low heat, stirring constantly until bubbly:

**¼ stick margarine**
**¼ cup all-purpose flour**
**½ teaspoon dry mustard**

Gradually add and stir:

**2½ cups milk**

Cook until thick and smooth, then add onions and peppers and:

**¼ teaspoon pepper**
**1½ cups shredded sharp Cheddar cheese**

Stir until cheese is melted, then stir in:

**2 cups chopped cooked Virginia or Country ham**

Alternate cheese sauce, sautéed onions and peppers in a lightly greased 2 quart casserole dish with layers of:

**6 cups thickly-sliced cooked potatoes**

Bake for 45 minutes. Top with:

**¼ cup grated Cheddar cheese**

Return to oven until cheese is melted.

# HAM AND RICE CASSEROLE

6 to 8 servings

Preheat oven to 350°. Beat in a small bowl:

    **1 egg**
    **1 cup milk**

Add to this mixture:

    **1 ten ounce can cream of
      celery soup**

Mix in another small bowl:

    **2 cups chopped cooked ham**
    **¼ teaspoon pepper**

Alternate in a greased casserole, with ham and soup mixture, so that there are double layers of each:

    **2 cups cooked rice**
    **¼ cup chopped onion**
    **¼ cup chopped green pepper**
    **1 can asparagus tips, drained**

Top with:

    **½ cup grated sharp Cheddar
      cheese**

Bake for 30 to 40 minutes.

# HAM AND WILD RICE CASSEROLE

In a large casserole, melt:

    **½ cup butter**

Add:

    **1½ cups uncooked wild rice**
    **1½ to 2 cups diced Country ham**
    **6 scallions, chopped**
    **1 cup sliced mushrooms**

Stir over low heat for ten minutes. Add:

    **2 ten ounce cans chicken
      consommé**
    **¾ cup white wine
      dash Tobasco
      dash marjoram**

Place in a greased casserole dish and bake at 375° for 1½ to 2 hours. Before serving, sprinkle with:

    **¼ cup grated Parmesan cheese**

# SQUASH AND HAM CASSEROLE

6 servings

Serve this as an accompaniment with sliced roast beef, fried chicken, or pork chops.

Preheat oven to 350°. Cook in unsalted water, if using Country ham, until tender and drain:

    **2 lbs. yellow squash, sliced**

Combine:

**2 eggs, beaten**
**¾ cup mayonnaise**
**1 small onion, chopped**
**½ cup chopped green pepper**
**1 cup grated Parmesan cheese**
**1 cup ground ham**
**¼ teaspoon pepper**

Mix with squash, and pour all ingredients into a buttered baking dish. Dot with:

**2 tablespoons butter**
**2 tablespoons bread crumbs or seasoned stuffing mix**
**2 tablespoons ground ham**

Bake 30 minutes.

---

## SWEET AND SOUR HAM

---

4 servings

Blend and refrigerate for 1 to 2 hours:

**1 pound cooked sugar-cured ham, cubed or 2 cups cubes**
**1½ teaspoons soy sauce**
**1 egg, beaten**
**½ teaspoon ginger powder**
**1 teaspoon red wine**
**½ teaspoon garlic powder**

Combine to form a batter the consistency of pancake batter:

**2 eggs**
**¼ cup cornstarch**

Dip cubes in batter and deep fry in oil for 2 minutes. Drain on paper towels. The ham cubes can be prepared ahead, then combined in a casserole dish with:

**¼ cup chopped green pepper in 1 inch pieces**
**1 cup pineapple chunks**
**½ cup chopped cooked carrots**

Pour *Sweet and Sour Sauce* over all and heat in a 350° oven for 20 minutes until heated through. Serve over regular rice or *Philippine Fried Rice*, omitting the ham.

---

## SWEET AND SOUR SAUCE

---

Combine and cook over medium heat until thickened:

**3 tablespoons white vinegar**
**½ teaspoon ginger powder**

**1 tablespoon cornstarch**
**1 teaspoon soy sauce**
**6 tablespoons sugar**
**3 tablespoons ketchup**
**1 cup pineapple juice**

# INTERNATIONAL COOKERY

Many countries around the world cure ham and use it as a main meat. The recipes included in this section are authentic native dishes of the countries decribed. A ham dish can be the center of attention at any foreign foods party, the inspiration for a costume affair, or to spice up a week of ordinary menus, try a ham dish with international flair.

# BITTERBALLEN

Makes 25

I acquired this recipe from a foreign exchange teacher from the Netherlands. It is a savory appetizer and well worth the time. People in the Netherlands serve this when drinking their Dutch Gin called Borrel, before dinner. But always serve the gin ice cold, but not with ice!

To make 1 cup of white sauce, melt over low heat:

**2 tablespoons butter**

Stir in:

**4 tablespoons flour**

Gradually add and blend until mixture thickens:

**1 cup milk**

Mix white sauce with:

**2 cups ground cooked ham**
**2 tablespoons minced parsley**
**2 tablespoons Worcestershire sauce**

Chill this mixture, shape into 1 inch balls and roll in:

**fine dry bread crumbs**

Mix:

**1 egg**
**1 tablespoon water**

Dip balls in egg mixture and again in the fine dry bread crumbs. Fry in hot fat (400°) for 1 to 2 minutes. Drain. Serve piping hot on wooden picks, with spicy mustard for dipping. These can be made ahead of time, then just put under the broiler until hot.

# SWEDISH HAM BALLS WITH BROWN SAUCE

Makes 36

Preheat oven to 325°. Combine:

**2 pounds ground ham**
**1 pound ground pork**
**2 eggs, well beaten**
**1 cup milk**
**1 heaping cup fine bread crumbs**

Mix and shape into 1-inch balls and place in an uncovered baking dish. Combine and stir over heat until sugar dissolves:

**1 cup brown sugar**
**½ cup vinegar**
**1 teaspoon dry mustard**
**½ cup water**

Pour over meat balls. Bake for 1½ to 2 hours. Baste every 20 minutes. Add more water to pan sauce, if needed. These can be made ahead and frozen; it's not necessary to thaw before cooking.

# SWEDISH CREPES WITH HAM FILLING

6 to 8 servings

Edna Brooks Turner, whose home is illustrated in the *Light Meals* chapter, is noted in Tidewater for her outstanding cooking parties. This is one of her favorite dishes that is suitable for any occasion. The dish freezes nicely; it can be made ahead and just reheated. They will melt in your mouth!

Make crepe batter by combining the following ingredients using a wire whisk:

> **3 eggs, slightly beaten**
> **1 cup plus 5 tablespoons flour**
> **2¼ cups milk and ¾ cup cream or**
> **2 cups half and half and**
> **1 cup milk**
> **¼ cup melted butter**
> **½ teaspoon salt**

Grease a 6 inch skillet or pan with butter; spoon into pan about 3 tablespoons of batter for each crepe, and tilt pan so batter will spread evenly over pan. Cook about 1 minute on each side until lightly brown. Remove crepe from pan and spread with a heaping spoonful of *Swedish Crepe Ham Filling*. Roll up and place crosswise in an oblong casserole dish. Repeat process with remaining batter and filling. Sprinkle filled crepes with:

> **Parmesan cheese**

Dot with:

> **butter**

When ready to serve, bake for 10 to 15 minutes in a preheated 425° oven until heated through.

# SWEDISH CREPE HAM FILLING

Mix together:

> **½ pound cooked Country ham, finely chopped**
> **½ pound mushrooms, sliced, or**
> **1 four ounce can sliced mushrooms, drained**
> **2 tablespoons chopped onion**
> **3 tablespoons butter, melted**
> **2 tablespoons flour**
> **1 cup cream**
> **1 tablespoon dry sherry**
> **¼ teaspoon pepper**

Spoon onto *Swedish Crepes* and bake as directed. An asparagus spear may be added to each crepe with filling and then rolled up. If you would like an alternate filling, try *Swedish Crepe Seafood Filling*.

# SWEDISH CREPE SEAFOOD FILLING

Combine and mix well:

- **1 pound cooked shrimp or crabmeat or combination**
- **2 tablespoons chives**
- **¼ cup butter**

- **2 tablespoons flour**
- **½ cup whipping cream**
- **½ cup milk**
- **1 egg yolk, slightly beaten**
- **1 tablespoon dry sherry**

# VEAL AND HAM PIE

4 to 6 servings

Meat pies are a traditional dish in the British Isles and Switzerland. They may be served warm or cold. For an intimate picnic serve sliced cold with Gruyere cheese and wine.

Preheat oven to 375°. Combine for a few minutes then drain:

- **2 slices bread, crumbled**
- **2 tablespoons milk**

In a large bowl combine with bread crumbs and mix well:

- **1½ cups ground cooked ham**
- **2 cups ground cooked veal**
- **1 tablespoon lemon juice**
- **1 teaspoon grated lemon peel**
- **1 teaspoon Worcestershire sauce**
- **1 medium onion, minced**
- **1 tablespoon finely chopped parsley flakes or ¼ cup finely chopped fresh parsley**
- **½ teaspoon salt (omit if ham is salty)**
- **½ teaspoon black pepper**
- **2 eggs, beaten**

Roll to about ⅛ inch thickness:

**Pastry Dough**

Use to line a greased 8 by 4 by 2½ inch loaf pan, letting the edge extend about ⅛ inch beyond the edge of the pan. Trim evenly. Spoon half the veal-ham mixture into the unbaked pastry; place in a line in the center of the mold:

**4 hard cooked eggs, peeled**

Top with rest of ham mixture. Place a rolled pastry covering on top of the loaf. Pinch bottom and top of the crust together. Brush pastry with:

**milk or beaten egg**

Bake for about 45 minutes to one hour or until golden brown. Let stand about 15 minutes before slicing. Serve with warmed sour cream and sprinkle with chives.

# PASTRY DOUGH

Measure into a bowl and blend:

**3 cups sifted flour**
**1 teaspoon salt**

Cut into flour:

**1 cup shortening**

Stir in, using as little as possible:

**10 to 12 tablespoons ice water**

Form into a ball, flatten and roll out on pastry cloth or floured counter top. For *Veal and Ham Pie,* divide in two balls before rolling out.

# MOUSSE AU JAMBON (Mousse with Ham)

The French are famous for the mousse, a light dish made from whipped cream, whites of eggs and various flavorings, either for dessert, lunch or appetizer. This ham mousse is perfect for a light lunch served with *Edna's Rolls* and fresh fruit. For the cocktail hour, let each guest help himself to a portion served on a cracker and topped with a thin sliver of cucumber.

Oil a one-quart mold lightly and invert on paper towel to drain. Sprinkle gelatin on top of liquid and set aside to soften for about 5 minutes:

**2 envelopes unflavored gelatin**
**¼ cup dry sherry or cold water**

In top of a double boiler beat until lemon colored:

**2 egg yolks**

Beat in:

**1 cup plus 5 tablespoons chicken stock**

Place top of double boiler over boiling water and cook, stirring constantly until mixture is thick enough to coat a spoon. Reduce heat to simmer and add the gelatin mixture and beat until it has completely dissolved. Stir in:

**3 cups ground cooked smoked ham or 1½ cups ground cooked Country ham**
**½ cup finely minced onion**
**½ teaspoon prepared horseradish (optional)**

Remove from heat and cool. Whip separately until soft peaks form:

**2 egg whites**
**1 cup heavy cream**

Fold into ham mixture, using a gentle motion so that the whites no longer show. Pour mousse into oiled mold. Smooth top with a spatula and chill until firm. To unmold mousse, run a small knife around the inside edge of the mold and dip the bottom of the mold in hot water for a few seconds. Place a chilled platter on top of the mold, invert, tap and mousse should slide out easily. Garnish with shredded lettuce or parsley and cocktail tomatoes. To form a ring, pour mousse into a lightly oiled ring mold and refrigerate until firm. Unmold as directed. Fill center with potato salad for a buffet. If any mousse is left, fill a scooped out cucumber with it, chill and slice for a special treat.

# CUSCINETTI DI VITELLO (Cushions of Veal)

8 servings

*Cuscinetti de Vitello* is Italian for small cushions of veal. They are stuffed with ham and cheese. When Marvin Seaman lived in Italy for two years he developed a real flair for preparing Italian dishes. This is one of his favorites.

Trim carefully and remove the bone from:

**2 pounds veal cutlets**

Pound the veal with a wooden mallet until quite thin. Cut into 16 four inch square scallops. Place on 8 of the squares, one per square:

**8 three inch squares thinly sliced Fontina or Gruyere cheese**

**8 three inch squares thinly sliced Prosciutto or cooked Country ham**

Top with the remaining veal scallops. The veal should cover the cheese and ham completely. Press the edges of the veal together and seal them by pounding with the flat of a cleaver or the side of a saucer. Season with:

**salt**
**freshly ground black pepper**

Dip each scallop in:

**flour**

Shake off the excess. In a heavy skillet, melt over moderate heat:

**2 tablespoons butter**
**3 tablespoons olive oil**

When the foam subsides, add the *cuscinetti*, three or four at a time, and cook in the hot fat, turning carefully until they are golden brown on both sides. As the *cuscinetti* are browned, transfer them to a platter. Discard most of the fat from the skillet, leaving a thin film on the bottom. Pour in:

**½ cup dry white wine**

Boil it briskly, stirring and scraping any browned bits that remain in the skillet, until the wine has been reduced by half. Add:

**½ cup chicken stock**

Bring it to a simmer. Then return the veal to the skillet. Cover. Simmer for twenty minutes over very low heat. Turn the *cuscinetti* over after 10 minutes. Transfer the *cuscinetti* to a heated serving platter. Add to the skillet:

**¼ cup chicken stock**
**¼ pound fresh mushrooms, sliced (optional)**

Bring the stock and pan juices to a boil for a minute or so. Season to taste with:

**salt and pepper**

Pour the sauce over the *cuscinetti* and serve.

# POLPETTONE

6 servings

This is a meat roll that my Italian friend, Grace Sibelius shared with me.

Preheat oven to 400°. Mix in a large bowl with a fork:

**1 pound ground round**
**1 egg**
  **dash salt**
  **dash pepper**
**4 tablespoons Parmesan cheese**
**1 teaspoon dried parsley or**
  **3 or 4 sprigs parsley**
**¼ teaspoon basil**

Flatten out meat mixture into an oval about ¾ inch thick. Slice:

**1 eight ounce package Mozzarella cheese**
**1 hard cooked egg**
**3 slices Prosciutto or cooked Country ham**

Arrange on the first third of the meat oval, one-third of the mozzarella, egg and ham. Starting at the end of the oval, roll the meat jelly-roll fashion over the layer of ingredients. Repeat layers of egg, cheese and ham. Continue to roll meat over ingredients. Repeat the third layer and make a final roll of the meat, shaping the loaf into an oblong (submarine shape) oval. Seal the edges of the meat roll with moistened hands. Grease baking dish or pan with:

**1½ teaspoons olive oil**

Coat meat roll with:

**1½ teaspoons olive oil**

Do not cover loaf. Bake for about 35 minutes. When it is golden brown, it is done. For a sauce you can pour 1 cup mashed canned tomatoes with juice over loaf before baking.

# PISELLI AL PROSCIUTTO (Braised Peas with Ham)

4 servings

In a heavy saucepan, melt over moderate heat:

**2 tablespoons butter**

Add and stir frequently until they are cooked soft but not brown:

**3 tablespoons finely chopped onion**

Stir in:

**2 cups fresh peas (2 pounds unshelled) or 1 ten ounce package frozen peas, defrosted**
**¼ cup chicken stock**

Cover and cook for 15 to 20 minutes until the peas are tender. Cut into 1 by ¼ inch julienne strips and add:

**2 ounces Prosciutto or cooked Country ham**

Cook uncovered, stirring frequently for about 2 minutes more or until all the liquid is absorbed. Taste for seasoning. Add as needed:

**salt**
**freshly ground black pepper**

Serve peas in a heated bowl; sprinkle with:

**1 tablespoon grated Parmesan cheese**

# PROSCIUTTO WITH MELON

4 servings

This is a traditional way to serve Italian ham, and it has become a classic appetizer, and dessert, around the world. This is delicious with a dinner featuring poultry or seafood.

Quarter:

**1 honeydew melon or cantaloupe**

On each wedge place one of:

**4 thin slices Prosciutto or
cooked Country ham**

# HAM RAGU BOLOGNESE STYLE SAUCE

Makes about 4 cups

Melt in a saucepan:

**2 tablespoons butter**

Sauté for about 10 minutes:

**½ cup chopped onion
¼ cup chopped celery
½ cup grated carrots
1 cup chopped mushrooms
1 cup chopped cooked ham**

In another skillet, stir until almost brown:

**¾ pound ground lean beef
dash salt**

Add and stir until brown:

**½ pound calf's liver, diced
dash salt**

Combine sautéed vegetables and meat.

Blend in:

**¼ cup tomato paste
1¼ cups dry white wine
1 cup water
½ cup beef stock
⅛ teaspoon pepper
¼ teaspoon nutmeg**

Simmer for 45 minutes. Stir in just before serving:

**1 cup whipping cream (optional)**

Serve over your favorite pasta such as egg noodles or spinach noodles. Marinated hearts of artichoke and lettuce salad served with *French Bread* completes this gourmet meal. You can use chicken livers in place of calf liver. Chop livers into small pieces, sauté them in butter until browned. Add to sauce 20 minutes before done.

# HAM RAGU WITH LASAGNE

6 servings

Preheat oven to 350°. Grease the bottom and sides of a 9 by 13 by 3 inch casserole with:

**butter**

In a large kettle, bring to a boil over high heat:

**6 quarts water**
**1 tablespoon salt**

Add:

**½ pound lasagne noodles**

Stir to keep noodles from sticking until tender, about 15 minutes. Place the pot under cold running water for a few minutes to cool the noodles. Lift out the lasagne strips carefully, and place on paper towels to drain. Prepare *besciamella* or cream sauce. Melt over low heat:

**3 tablespoons butter**

Add:

**6 tablespoons flour**

Add and stir until smooth:

**2 cups milk**
**1 cup heavy cream**

Place pan back on medium heat and constantly stir until thickened. A wire whisk is helpful. Season to taste with:

**salt**
**pepper**
**nutmeg**

Spread a layer of *Ham Ragu Bolognese Style Sauce,* omitting whipping cream, about ¼ inch deep in bottom of casserole. Spread over ragu about 1 cup of cream sauce. Layer about one-third of the lasagne noodles, overlapping them slightly on top of the sauce. Repeat these layers until the dish is filled, topping the last with ragu and cream sauce. Spread on top:

**grated Parmesan cheese**

Bake until bubbly, about 30 minutes.

# ITALIAN HAM CABBAGE ROLLS

8 servings

Preheat oven to 350°. Immerse in a large kettle of boiling water for about 3 minutes until limp, then drain:

**8 large cabbage leaves**

Combine:

**1 cup partially cooked rice**
**2 cups ground cooked ham**
**1 medium onion, chopped fine**
**½ teaspoon pepper**
**1 teaspoon parsley**
**½ cup grated Parmesan cheese**

**1 beaten egg**

Place 2 large tablespoons of mixture on each cabbage leaf. Roll up as if wrapping a package and place in a casserole dish, seam sides down.

Make sauce by mixing:

**2 cups tomato sauce**
**2 tablespoons minced onion**
**1 teaspoon Italian seasoning**

Pour over cabbage rolls. Bake, covered, for 1½ hours.

# HAM AND POTATOES WITH AN AUSTRIAN FLAIR

6 servings

This recipe comes from Missy Aue, whose husband is from Vienna, Austria. Missy was a home economics major at Madison College. This is nice with a salad of romaine, red lettuce, chilled orange sections, and water chestnut slices with Italian dressing.

Cook 5 minutes on each side in a heavy frying pan:

**8 ounces Country ham, sliced**

Remove ham and trim all fat. Return fat to pan and cook slowly. Cut ham into fine julienne pieces. Combine and add to pan drippings:

**3 ounces vinegar**
**2 tablespoons water**
**1 beaten egg**
**1 teaspoon sugar**
**1 teaspoon salt (omit if ham is salty)**
**¼ teaspoon pepper**

Stir until thickened over low heat. Add and mix well:

**4 cups sliced cooked potatoes**
**½ cup chopped onion**

Add ham strips, heat thoroughly and serve.

# HEISER KARTOFFEL SALAT MIT SCHINKEN
## [Hot Potato Salad With Ham]

4 servings

My German friend Frances Haas is a charming lady fondly known to all the children in Chuckatuck Village as Ma Ma Pa. She is a real grandmama to all and it is always a treat to visit her in hopes to sample her excellent cooking and see what new herb is growing in her well-tended garden. Germans, she says, do not like to waste anything and when cooking with ham she doesn't waste even a crumb. She utilizes every morsel in her two most frequently made ham dishes...noodles with ham and potato salad. The German people traditionally eat their potato salad hot, however you may chill if you prefer.

Scrub and rinse:

**3 to 4 medium potatoes**

Boil in jackets; cool enough to handle, then peel and cut into ¼ inch slices. Place in a skillet and cook on medium for a few minutes:

**¼ cup diced ham fat**

Add to hot grease and sauté until tender:

**1 medium sized onion, chopped**
**½ cup chopped cooked ham**

Add and let come to a boil:

**¼ cup vinegar**
**½ cup beef or chicken stock or bouillon**
**¼ teaspoon pepper**
**salt to taste**
**1 teaspoon sugar**

Remove from heat and pour over potatoes. Serve hot.

## SCHINKEN MIT NUDELN (Ham with Noodles)

4 to 6 servings

Preheat oven to 350°. Cook according to directions:

**1 eight ounce package
egg noodles**

Drain and wash in cold water to prevent being sticky. Layer in a greased casserole dish, alternating layers of noodles and:

**about 2 cups chopped cooked ham**

Place in oven for 15 minutes. Meanwhile combine:

**3 eggs, well beaten
1 cup sour cream**

At the end of 15 minutes cooking time, pour egg mixture over noodles. Bake 15 minutes more. Serve. This is good with a tossed salad. Mix oil, vinegar and chopped onions, with salt and pepper to taste, pour over the salad and serve at once.

## HAM AND BARLEY SOUP

8 servings

This is an old Czechoslovakian recipe that has been passed down for several generations in the Lovich family. It makes a hearty soup, and if you're lucky enough to have any left, it can be stored in the refrigerator for several days.

Place in pot:

**2 quarts water**

**1 hambone with small pieces of
ham**

Cook about 1 hour and then add:

**½ cup catsup
1 cup barley**

Cook until barley is soft and add:

**2 cups cooked diced potatoes
dash of salt, if needed**

Simmer until heated through and serve.

# MIDDLE EASTERN STUFFED GRAPE LEAVES

24 servings

Secure:

**24 medium grape leaves**

Rinse in cold water, then soak in hot water for 15 minutes. Squeeze out excess water. Combine and mix well:

**1 pound cooked lamb or beef, chopped fine**
**1 cup finely minced cooked ham**
**1 cup uncooked rice, rinsed**
**¼ teaspoon pepper**
**½ teaspoon salt (omit if ham is salty)**

Spoon 2 tablespoons of mixture on each grape leaf, tuck in ends and roll away from you. Line the bottom of a heavy pan with:

**4 chicken necks or wings or lamb bones**

This prevents scorching; a wire rack may be used. Arrange stuffed grape leaves over bones or rack, press an inverted dish on top and fill the pan with water to reach the dish. Cook 35 minutes on low heat or until tender. During the last 10 minutes of cooking add:

**juice from 2 lemons**

# MEXICAN SPAGHETTI

6 to 8 servings

Preheat oven to 350°. Boil according to package directions:

**1 seven ounce package spaghetti**

Fry:

**6 slices bacon**

Place on paper towels and set aside. In bacon drippings brown:

**1 pound ground hamburger**
**1 small onion, diced**

Add:

**½ pound minced cooked ham**

Mix with the browned meats and spaghetti:

**½ green pepper, diced**
**1 four ounce can pimiento, diced**
**1 garlic clove, diced**
**1 teaspoon paprika**
**½ teaspoon salt (omit if ham is salty)**
**½ teaspoon pepper**
**1 no. 303 can stewed tomatoes**
**1 no. 303 can garden peas, undrained**

Place in a 3 quart baking dish. Cover with the fried bacon and:

**½ pound sharp Cheddar cheese, grated**

Bake, covered, for 1 hour. Uncover; bake until bacon is crisp.

# CHILIES RELLENOS VIRGINIA

4 servings

Carol Fontaine Frohman adapted this colorful Mexican dish.

Carefully remove seeds and ribs from:

**4 small green chili peppers**

Parboil peppers about 8 minutes, drain. Cut into strips about the same size as peppers:

**4 sticks Monterey Jack or Swiss cheese**

**2 slices cooked ham**

Stuff the peppers with the cheese and ham. Separate:

**2 eggs**

In a small bowl beat the yolks and in another bowl, beat whites until they hold soft peaks. Gently fold yolks into whites using an under-and-over motion. Add:

**2 tablespoons flour**

Continue to fold in until no white spots are visible. In a deep fat fryer or skillet, heat 3 inches of oil to 400°. While oil is heating, roll the ham and cheese stuffed peppers in:

**flour**

With a large cooking spoon dip peppers in batter, coating them generously. Place peppers in hot fat and fry until golden on all sides, 3 to 4 minutes. Serve *Chilies Rellenos Sauce Virginia.*

# CHILIES RELLENOS SAUCE VIRGINIA

**1 pound can stewed tomatoes**
**2 tablespoons finely chopped onion**
**½ teaspoon salt**

**¼ teaspoon dried oregano leaves**
**dash pepper**

Simmer, stirring occasionally, for 10 minutes. Serve over peppers.

# PARAGUAYAN PASTA

8 servings

This is hearty and your guests will love it, says my friend Grace Leach, who serves this for party buffets. A green salad and *French Bread* will complete the meal.

Preheat oven to 350°. Fry until crisp:

**3 slices bacon**

Drain on paper towels, then crumble and set aside. In bacon drippings sauté lightly:

**1 medium onion, chopped**
**1 cup cooked ham, cut in strips**
**2 Spanish sausages, thinly sliced**
**or ¼ pound hot Italian sausage**
**and ¼ pound mild Italian**
**sausage, thinly sliced**

Add:

**1 eight ounce can tomato sauce**

**1 tomato, chopped**
**¼ teaspoon pepper**
**1 teaspoon salt (omit if ham is**
**salty)**

Cover and simmer for 20 minutes. Add along with crumbled bacon and simmer for 15 minutes more:

**1 cup sliced mushrooms**
**1 cup beef bouillon**

In a large casserole dish, arrange, and alternate layers of sauce and:

**1 pound package Rollini noodles,**
**cooked**
**½ cup Mozzarella cheese**
**½ cup Parmesan cheese**

End layers with sauce and cheese. Bake for 25 minutes or until lightly browned.

# LEBANESE HAM-STUFFED CABBAGE ROLLS

Makes 12 to 15 servings

Cut core from:

**1 large or 2 medium heads**
**cabbage**

Drop head of cabbage, core first, in salted boiling water for about 5 to 10 minutes until leaves are softened and wilted; do not get too soft or cabbage leaf will fall apart when rolled with stuffing. Remove, place on a dish or paper towel to drain and cool. Remove leaves from cabbage and cut heavy rib from each end of the leaf.

To make stuffing, combine:

**1 pound ground lamb or lean beef**
**1 cup cooked ham, chopped fine**
**1 cup rice, uncooked but rinsed**
**well**
**¼ teaspoon salt**
**¼ teaspoon pepper**
**1 teaspoon allspice**

Spoon about 2 tablespoons stuffing onto each leaf and roll up cigar fashion. In the bottom of a heavy saucepan, place a few lamb bones or chicken wings—if you have them on hand; if not place the ribs removed from the cabbage leaves on the bottom. Place the stuffed leaves on top of the bones, wings or ribs. This prevents the leaves from sticking.

Mix and pour over rolls:

**1 pound can tomatoes, mashed**
**½ teaspoon salt**

Arrange in each corner of dish:

**2 cloves garlic, cut in half**

Sprinkle over top:

**½ teaspoon dried mint**

Place an inverted dish on cabbage rolls to hold them down, cover and cook on medium heat about 25 minutes. Add:

**juice from 2 lemons**

Cook 10 minutes more and serve.

## NICK'S HAM STUFFED FLANK STEAK

4 to 6 servings

Preheat oven to 325°. Trim fat and about ½ cup steak scraps from:

**1½ to 2 pounds flank steak**

Chop the fat and steak trimmings very fine and set aside. With a sharp knife make a pocket inside the flank steak to hold the stuffing. On both sides of the steak sprinkle lightly:

**salt and pepper**

Place steak in an oblong baking dish. Prepare stuffing:

**2 cups finely chopped fresh
   mushrooms or 1 cup canned
   mushrooms, drained**
**1 clove garlic, finely minced**
**½ cup finely minced celery**

**1 cup finely chopped cooked ham**
**½ cup finely minced onion**

Sauté this, along with the ½ cup steak trimmings, until golden brown in:

**3 tablespoons butter**

Spoon stuffing into pocket. Close with miniature skewers or toothpicks. Pour over the steak:

**1 eight ounce can tomato sauce**

Cut in 4 pieces:

**1 garlic bulb**

Place a piece in each corner of the casserole dish. Bake for 1 hour. Cool for at least 10 minutes before serving; slice to serve. If stuffing falls apart, just spoon onto plate. Spoon a little sauce over each serving.

# PHILIPPINE FRIED RICE

8 servings

My friend Toni Gardy lived in the Philippines for several years. She adapted this traditional island dish to suit the American taste. It is served as part of the meal, but when served with a green vegetable and a salad this actually makes a complete meal.

Cook according to package directions:

**1 fourteen ounce box quick cooking rice**

Drain and refrigerate for several hours or overnight; this prevents the rice from becoming too mushy when fried. Fry:

**6 slices bacon**

Drain on paper towel, then crumble and set aside. Sauté in bacon drippings until golden and crunchy, taking care not to overcook:

**1 cup diced cooked ham**
**1 large pepper, chopped**
**4 carrots, diced**
**1 cup celery, sliced diagonally**

Beat together:

**1 large egg**
**1 teaspoon soy sauce**
**¼ teaspoon pepper**

Add to vegetable mixture. Fry until egg is soft. Add cooked rice and crumbled bacon, stir until heated completely through. Serve hot!

# MORCON

8 to 10 servings

Did you ever think *ham* would be your inspiration for a Philippine dinner? By using only ½ cup ham combined with other delectable ingredients, you can enjoy this authentic meat roll that Mrs. Letti delRosahio, a Philippine friend, gave me.

Pound with a meat tenderizing mallet to ¼ inch thickness, 12 by 16 inches:

**1½ pounds lean boneless sirloin or round steak**

Spread out beef and season with:

**dash pepper**
**dash salt**

Make a vinegar solution by combining:

**¼ cup wine vinegar**
**2 cloves garlic, mashed**
**10 peppercorns, crushed**

Soak beef in this mixture for 20 minutes. Cut into strips:

**½ cup cooked ham**
**4 slices uncooked bacon**
**2 pieces Vienna sausage**

Combine with:

**12 olives, sliced**

Drain beef, reserving marinade, spread flat and top with ham mixture. Arrange down the center of the ham mixture:

2 hard-cooked eggs, halved

Roll meat in jelly-roll fashion and tie with a string. Melt in a large pan:

¼ cup shortening

Fry meat roll until brown. Add along with marinade:

1 quart water
½ bay leaf
1 medium onion, chopped

3 tomatoes, diced
½ teaspoon salt

Simmer until tender, about 1 hour. Add:

1 cup tomato sauce

Continue to cook for 5 more minutes. Remove roll. Cool 10 minutes, remove string, slice crosswise and serve with the sauce.

---

# HAM FRIED RICE HONG WOO

---

8 servings

Cook as directed on package:

2 cups rice
2 chicken bouillon cubes

Sauté:

1 cup sliced ham, cut in diagonal strips
1 ounce peanut oil

Remove ham from pan. Sauté:

1 cup diagonally sliced celery
1 large onion, sliced diagonally

1 eight ounce can water chestnuts, sliced thinly

Add ham to sauteed vegetables. Beat together:

3 large eggs
1 teaspoon soy sauce
¼ teaspoon pepper

Pour into vegetable and ham mixture. Stir and fry until soft. Add:

2 green onions, including tops, minced

Add cooked rice, mix well, serve hot.

# CHINESE EGGROLL

Makes 8 large or 24 small

To make batter for eggroll wrappers, slightly beat:

**2 eggs**

Beat into the eggs:

**1 cup all purpose flour**
**2 tablespoons cornstarch**
**½ teaspoon salt**
**2 cups water**

Heat a greased 7 or 8 inch cast iron skillet or crepe pan over medium heat until just hot, not smoking. Pour one tablespoon of batter in pan, quickly tilt so batter covers the pan thinly and evenly. Cook about one minute until it is done. Lift edge to test for doneness. These eggroll wrappers may be frozen as soon as cool enough; having them ready ahead of time helps. For the filling, mix:

**1 egg**

**1 cup chopped cooked shrimp, crabmeat or lobster**
**½ cup finely chopped celery**
**¼ cup minced cooked ham**
**¼ cup chopped water chestnuts**
**¼ cup bamboo shoots**
**1 tablespoon soy sauce**
**2 tablespoons minced green onion**

Shape mixture into finger sized rolls. Lay on cooked side of eggroll wrapper and fold left and right side over the filling. Slivered cabbage can be added for bulk if desired. Fold edge nearest you over filling and continue to roll. Carefully seal the end by brushing the exposed edge with egg or uncooked batter. Brush the eggroll with beaten egg. Place eggroll in 2 inches of hot oil (375°). Cook until golden brown on both sides; drain well. Keep warm in the oven. Serve with either of the following *Sweet and Sour Sauces*.

# SWEET AND SOUR SAUCE I

Put into saucepan:

**1 cup pineapple cubes**
**1 green pepper, cut into squares**
**½ cup vinegar**
**¼ cup packed brown sugar**
**¾ cup water**

**1 tablespoon molasses**

Mix well and add to saucepan:

**2 tablespoons cornstarch**
**¼ cup water**

Slowly bring to boil, stirring constantly. Serve hot or cold.

# SWEET AND SOUR SAUCE II

Pour into a saucepan:

**1 cup sweet pickle juice**

Mix well and add to saucepan:

**1 tablespoon cornstarch**
**⅛ cup water**

Heat until thickened, then serve.

# ACKNOWLEDGEMENTS

We are very appreciative of all the dedicated staff at Donning, especially Donna and Bob Friedman and Ed Conner. In acknowledgement of our faithful typist, Connie Bunch, and to our many friends whose valuable contributions have made this book possible, thank you.

Nita Alphin
Ms. Morton Asbury
Mrs. William Aue
Mrs. Rudolph Badger
Mrs. Douglas Baker
Allie Baker
Mrs. I. M. Baker, Jr.
Ida Barnes
Mrs. Richard Baylor
Sarah Beaty
Mrs. John P. Beneke
Mr. and Mrs. Charles S. Betts, Jr.
Mrs. George Birdsong
Mrs. Ray Blanton
Mrs. George Blair
Mrs. Charles Bolt
Mrs. David Bonner
J. P. Boone
Mrs. Lee Bowman
Mrs. Roy Van Brinkley
Betsy Brothers
Mrs. Ray Buck
Mrs. Herman W. Bunch, Jr.
Mrs. P. M. Burton
Mrs. George Busbee
Sarah Butler
Mrs. Jimmy Carter
Robert Carpenter
Charlann Carroll
Bonnie Cavender
Martha Cherry
Eleanor Clarke
Mrs. F. O. Clarke
Mary Stallings Cooley
Josephine Copeland
Edna Craighead
Jean Cross
Segar Cofer Dashiell
Letti del Rosario
Elizabeth Dixon
Mrs. J. C. Draper, Jr.
Mrs. George B. Duke
Mrs. John D. Eure, Jr.
Robert Everett
Mrs. William Everett
Mrs. Albert W. Farrenkopf, Jr.
Mrs. C. M. Flintoff
Mrs. Gerald Ford
Mrs. Daniel C. Frohman
Mrs. David Frohman
Nita Fry
Mrs. Norman E. Fussell

Mrs. Jeffrey Gardy
Brooks Godwin
Mrs. Mills E. Godwin, Jr.
Sally Gray
Mrs. Howard Gwaltney, Jr.
Howard Gwaltney, Sr.
P. D. Gwaltney, III
Frances Haas
Hattie L. Hale
Ellen Hallock
Mary Hancock
Elizabeth J. Harrell
Robyn Herr
Iva Herring
Mrs. James E. Holshouser, Jr.
Mrs. Garland E. Hines, Jr.
Mrs. Quimby Hines, Sr.
Mr. and Mrs. Quimby Hines, Jr.
Mrs. David L. Hopewell, Jr.
Mrs. Dillard Horton, Jr.
Laura House
Mrs. Robert V. House
George Howerton
Edith Hurff
Jean Jones
Martha Jones
Barbara Joyner
Mrs. Edward Joyner
Mrs. Donald Keyt
Nancy King
Rosa Lamb
Nancy Lane
Grace Leach
Madeline Lovelace
Mrs. Joe Lovich
Emily Harrell Lynch
Etta Mabry
Mrs. Jack D. Mahan
Pearson Mapes
Iris McCotter
Mrs. Charles McElroy
Susan Milburn
Mrs. Andrew Miller
Mrs. George Miller
Kathryn Mitchell
Mrs. Raymond Mize
Patrick Montgomery
Mrs. Henry Murden
Sue Harrell Nichols
Lundy Nicholson
Mildred Norwood
Nick Otto

Mrs. Bathurst D. Peachy, Jr.
Mrs. William S. Peachy
Olivia Pert
Jim Pittman
Tonia Phillips
Beth Polson
Mrs. Richard Pond
Mrs. Carroll Preece
Mrs. Peter Pruden, Jr.
Martha Pruden
Mrs. John C. Ramsey, Jr.
Mrs. Larry Riddick
James Monroe Roberson, Sr.
Mamie Roberson
Dr. Dorothy Rowe
Mrs. W. G. Saunders, Jr.
Mrs. Thomas Savage
Petronia Schloss
Marvin R. Seaman
Mrs. David W. Shaw
Mrs. Charles H. Shotton
Mrs. Douglas Shotton
Grace Sibelius
Martha Sieg
Mrs. Edward D. Smith
Smithfield Packing Company
Joann Spivey
Mrs. Jack Stain
Mr. and Mrs. Roger Steinbach
St. John's Episcopal Church Parish
Mrs. Walter F. Story
Mrs. John Taylor
Nat Thompson
Minnielee Toler
Richard L. Turner
Edna Brooks Saunders Turner
Susan Villiard
Churchill Young
Mrs. Wallace Walton
Mr. and Mrs. Frank M. Warrington
Kit Webb
Cecil L. Webb
Mrs. James M. Weiss
Charlotte Whetzle
Carolyn White
Lee White
Sandra Whitt
Roberta Wills
Susan E. Winborne
Dr. Hong Woo
Ginger Woo
Gladys Yates

# INDEX